Law and Gospel
by
Dr Kristina Howells

Printed in the European Union

All Scripture quotations come from the English Heritage Bible and KJV.
All artwork in this book other than sources mentioned are done by Dr Kristina Howells

ISBN 978-1-8479962-1-3

For additional copies please order online at:
www.lulu.com

DEDICATION

This book is dedicated to all my friends and family who have supported me in this work.

A special mention also goes to Dr Gwin Turner President of Cathedral University who has now sadly passed away for his help and support in proof reading this book.

Proverbs 18:24; *"A man may be good for nothing to his friends, and there is a friend who sticks like a brother."*

Contents page

Introduction

This book has been written to reflect on the Law and Gospel and how the Ten Commandments are relevant to our walk with the Lord. The different categories of Law which will be looked at are how the law is defined in the bible, God's law in today's society, as well as God's law in men's hearts.

However, we do need to fully understand the importance of the Law and Gospel; this will be looked at in detail, which will conclude with understanding the Law and Gospel, the law and Jesus, the spirit of life and finally Calvin on the Law and the Gospel.

The Law of God is vital for our very existence in both this world and the world to come. Jesus came to fulfil the Law, as he says in Matthew 5:17-19;
17 Do not suppose that I came to loosen down the law or the prophets; I absolutely did not come to loosen down, but to fulfil.
18 Because, Amen, I say to you, Until heaven and earth pass away, one iota or one particle will absolutely not pass away from the law until all comes to be.
19 Whoever therefore will make one of these least commandments loose, and teaches men in this way, he shall be called the least in the kingdom of heaven, and whoever does and teaches them, this one will be called great in the kingdom of heaven.

Therefore what the scripture tells us clearly here is that we are all subjected to the law and to the judgments. Jesus in these words says that ministers of His Word who teach that the Law of God as given to Moses is not important will be called least in the kingdom of heaven, and those who teach the Law of God as given to Moses will be called great in the kingdom of heaven.

There are far too many of God's ministers who have taken a non-biblical view of Paul's teachings, and taught either directly or by their neglect that God's Law as given to Moses is not applicable today. Many preach only the "New" Testament, and consider the "Old" Testament as not important. They neither study it, nor preach it. The reason is that they do not understand what Jesus did.

Jesus states very clearly that He did not come to loosen down the law, but to fulfil it, Matthew 5:17 and further declares that not one iota or one particle will pass away until all comes to be – not only in the life of Jesus, but also in the life of the believer, as well as ultimately in the new heaven and the new earth.

We cannot be saved by keeping the Law, because no one has ever lived perfect on this earth except Jesus. That is why Jesus came, to do what we could not do - to do that for us. Upon taking Him, His Holy Spirit creates within us a new spirit and nature, and enables us to obey His law.

Only the most deceived would argue that we are exempt from obeying the Ten Commandments since we have become Christians. As a new born believers we are not now free to commit adultery, steal, and violate all the rest of God's commandments, because Jesus fulfilled the Law for us, Rom 6:1; *"What therefore shall we speak? Shall we stay in sin that grace may super- abound?"*

We need to understand that there is one Law, God's Law. There never have been two, nor will there ever be. The same Law of God given to Israel is the same Law given to all, and applicable to all, Num 15:16; *"One law and one judgment shall be for you and for the stranger who lodges with you."*

The law of Jehovah is complete, converting the soul, Psalm 19:7; *"The law of Jehovah is complete, converting the soul; the testimony of Jehovah is faithful, making the open wise."*

The Law of Moses only claimed completeness or perfection in the coming of the Messiah to pour out His blood in the perfect sacrifice to fulfil every detail prophesied in the Law of Moses. The error the Pharisees and others espoused in Jesus' day was that they thought that their outward efforts to outwardly conform to God's Law would save them, rejecting the Holy Spirit conviction that they had not been able to perfectly keep God's Law even outwardly much less in their hearts, and rejecting God's Messiah who was the fulfilment of every Law of sacrificial blood ever pictured in any animal sacrifice, as well as perfectly fulfilling the moral law, and all the rest of the law.

There is only one Law, but for purposes of understanding the Law it can be divided into the moral Law, the ceremonial Law, the civil Law, and the health Law. We are more responsible for the moral Law today than ever before because of its complete fulfilment and revelation in the life of Jesus, and our receiving a holy nature enabling us to live it out in our lives.

The ceremonial Law was fulfilled to the last detail in the Lord Jesus, and we reap its blessings in the present Priestly ministry of the Lord Jesus, and His shed blood now effective in the Holy of Holies in heaven, where we are to boldly enter constantly to receive grace, Heb 10:19; *"Having therefore, brothers, outspokenness for entrance into the sanctuary in the blood of Jesus"*

The civil Law which God gave to govern Israel, to protect the innocent, to punish the guilty, and to control the spread of lawlessness and chaos, is perfect, and far superior to the laws of any modern government.

The health Law given by God to maintain health by eating habits, and washings to cleanse away disease and maintain health, and obedience to, and faith in, all of God's moral, civil, and spiritual laws to receive and maintain healing, is far superior to any medical science anywhere in the modern world.

So we do not quote Paul that we are not under law, but under grace, Rom 6:14; *"Because sin will absolutely not lord it over you, because you are absolutely not under the law, but under grace."*
Amen

Law and Gospel

Rom. 3:21-31;
21 And now the righteousness of God apart from the law has been manifested, being witnessed by the law and the prophets,
22 And the righteousness of God through Jesus Christ's faith is to all, and upon all those believing, because there is absolutely no variation,
23 Because all have sinned, and lack the glory of God;
24 Being justified freely by his grace through the redemption in Christ Jesus,
25 Whom God has set forth to be a covering through faith in his blood, to a display of his righteousness through the passing over of sins previously transpired in the forbearance of God,
26 For the display of his righteousness in the present time, into his being righteous and justifying the one who is of Jesus' faith.
27 Where therefore is boasting? It is shut out. Through what law? Of works? Absolutely not, but through the law of faith.
28 Therefore we calculate that a man is justified by faith apart from law works.
29 Or is he the God of the Jews only? And is he absolutely not also of the races? Yes, also of the races.
30 Since indeed there is one God who will justify the circumcision out of faith and the uncircumcision through faith,
31 Therefore do we render the law inoperative through faith? We do not! On the contrary, we cause the law to stand.

This scripture tells us that we are saved by God's grace, through faith alone, apart from the works of the law.

However, there are many amongst us that question justification is by grace alone, but it is also through faith and the righteousness of Christ. But it is one notion to distinguish between faith and works, and a different notion to distinguish law and gospel.

What is the Traditional Distinction?

The traditional distinction applies to the false and the true way of salvation. That are defined in the Gospel as being two messages, one that consists of commands, threats, and therefore terrors, and the other that consists of promises and comforts.

We are saved entirely by God's grace and not by works, we can see clearly in the bible that there are two different messages of God in the Scripture, one is of command ("law") and the other is of promise ("Gospel").

In Scripture itself, commands and promises are found together. With God's promises there are also commands to repent of sin and believe the promise. The commands are not merely announcements of judgment, but God's grace upon us to repent of sin and believe in him.

As the Psalmist says, *"be gracious to me through your law,"* Psalm. 119:29.

Mark 1:15; *"And saying, The time has been fulfilled, and the kingdom of God is drawing near; repent, and believe in the good news"*

Acts 14:15; *"And saying, Men, why are you doing these things? We also are men of like feelings as you, announcing the good news to you to turn from these empty things to the living God, who made the heaven, and the earth, and the sea, and all things in them,"*

Acts 20:21; *"Solemnly witnessing both to the Jews, and also to the Greeks, repentance toward God, and faith toward our Lord Jesus Christ."*

Many preachers take these two passages when preaching the command to repent of sin as an importance in their sermons.

Where are the Law and Gospel in Scripture?

The New Testament is the good news that the kingdom of God has come in Jesus and that He had come to fulfil the law.

Matt. 4:23, *"And Jesus went around the whole of Galilee, teaching in their synagogues, and preaching the good news of the kingdom, and healing every sickness and every weakness in the people."*

Matt. 5:17, *"Do not suppose that I came to loosen down the law or the prophets; I absolutely did not come to loosen down, but to fulfill."*

Matt 9:35, *"And Jesus went around all the cities and villages teaching in their synagogues, and preaching the good news of the kingdom, and healing every sickness and every weakness in the people."*

Mark 1:14, *"And after that John was given over into prison, Jesus came into Galilee, preaching the good news of the kingdom of God."*

Luke 4:43, *"And he said to them, Because also I must announce the good news of the kingdom of God to other cities, because I was set apart and sent for this."*

Acts 20:24, *"But I make absolutely no word of it, and I absolutely do not hold my soul precious to myself, so that I may finish my race with joy, and the ministry, which I took alongside of the Lord Jesus, to solemnly witness to the good news of the grace of God."*

What is God's Kingdom?

God's Kingdom is:-

1. God's sovereign power,
2. His sovereign authority,
3. His coming to defeat Satan and bring about salvation,
4. God's power including the Resurrection of Christ.

God's authority is the constant reiteration of his commandments. When the power of God's kingdom appears, it is time for people to repent. We must obey the Gospel.

2 Thess. 1:8, *"In flaming fire giving vengeance to those not seeing God, and those not attentively hearing the good news of our Lord Jesus Christ."*

1 Pet. 4:17, *"Because it is time to begin the judgment from the house of God, and if it first begins*

from us, what will be the end of those not being convinced of the good news of God?"

The Gospel requires a certain kind of conduct; we must obey the word of God.

Acts 14:15; *"And saying, Men, why are you doing these things? We also are men of like feelings as you, announcing the good news to you to turn from these empty things to the living God, who made the heaven, and the earth, and the sea, and all things in them."*

Gal. 2:14; *"But when I saw that they absolutely did not walk uprightly with the truth of the good news, I said to Peter in front of all, If you, being a Jew, live as one of another race, and absolutely not as Jews, why do you constrain the races to be Jews?"*

Phil. 1:27; *"Only let your behaviour as a citizen be worthy of the good news of Christ, that whether I come and see you, or whether I am away, I hear the things concerning you, that you stand firm in one spirit, with one soul wrestling together for the faith of the good news."*

Rom 2:16; *"In the day when God will judge the secrets of men by Jesus Christ according to my good news."*

God brings his power and authority to bear on all of his creatures. In His kingdom, He establishes peace.

Eph. 6:15; *"And having put shoes on the feet in the preparation of the good news of peace."*

Acts 10:36; *"The word which he set apart and sent to the children of Israel, announcing the good news of peace through Jesus Christ (he is Lord of all)."*

Rom. 10:15; *"And how may they preach, if they have not been set apart and sent? As it has been written, How beautifully timely are the feet of them who announce the good news of peace, those announcing the good news of inherent good things!"*

The Gospel shows us how God brings Gentiles and Jews together in one body.

Rom. 16:25; *"And to the one having power to set you steadfast according to my good news, and the preaching of Jesus Christ, according to the revelation of the mystery, having been kept silent since the eternal ages."*

Eph. 6:19; *"And for me, that the word may be given to me, in opening my mouth in outspokenness, to make known the mystery of the good news."*

God's power is to save, and that is also by the reiteration of God's commands, and His coming to execute his plan, that is the Gospel. It is good news to know that God is bringing "His plans to fruition."

In Isa. 52:7; *"How beautiful upon the mountains are the feet of him who announces good tidings, who causes peace to be attentively heard, who announces good tidings of good, who causes salvation to be attentively heard, who says to Zion, Your God reigns!"*

This is one of the most important passages of the New Testament in terms of the Gospel: It is the reign of God that is good news, news that ensures peace and salvation. Even the demand for repentance is good news, because it shows that God is willing to forgive for Christ's sake.

However, the Gospel includes law as important: God's authority, his demand to repent. Even on the view of those most committed to the law and the Gospel, and more importantly the Gospel commands us to believe.

It requires faith as well, as faith itself works through love,

Gal. 5:6; *"Because in Christ Jesus absolutely neither circumcision has strength for anything, nor uncircumcision, but faith supernaturally working through love."*

And is dead without good works

James 2:17; *"In this way, faith, if it does not have works, by itself is dead."*

Having faith does not mean that you are saved or merit salvation, any more than any other human act merits salvation. Thus when we speak of faith, it is not based just on the ground of salvation, but as the instrument.

Faith saves, not because one merits salvation, but because it reaches out to receive God's grace in Christ. Nevertheless, faith is an obligation, as well as the command to believe.

It is also true that law is included in the Gospel. God gives us his law as part of a covenant, and that covenant is a gift of God's grace. As it is written, *"I am the Lord your God, who brought you out of the land of Egypt, out of the house of slavery."*

It is only after Israel proclaimed His saving grace that God then issues his commands to Israel, by offering Israel a new way of life, conferred by His grace.

Deut. 7:7-8; *"Jehovah did not join you to himself in love because you were more abundant than all peoples, or choose you because you were the fewest of all people, Because of Jehovah's love to you, and because he hedged about the oath which he swore to your fathers, Jehovah has brought you out with a strong hand, and redeemed you out of the house of servants, from the hand of Pharaoh, king of Egypt."*

Deut 9:4-6; *"Do not say in your heart, after that Jehovah, your God, has pushed them out from before your face, saying, Jehovah has brought me in to possess this land for my righteousness; but Jehovah drives them out from before your face for the wickedness of these peoples.*
5 You go to possess their land, not for your righteousness, or for the uprightness of your heart, but Jehovah, your God, possesses them from before your face because of the wickedness of these peoples, and that he may cause the word to rise up which Jehovah swore to your fathers, Abraham, Isaac, and Jacob.
6 You shall know by seeing that Jehovah, your God, is not giving you this good land to possess for your righteousness, because you are a stiff-necked people."

Does the command of God refer to the "law" or "gospel?"

We can see that it is both for we are told in Ex. 20:18-21; *"And all the people saw the voices, and the flames, and the voice of the trumpet, and the mountain smoking; and when the people saw, they vacillated back and forth, and stood afar off.*
19 And they said to Moses, You speak with us, and we will attentively hear; and do not let God speak with us lest we die.
20 And Moses said to the people; Do not fear, because God has come in order to test you, and that his fear may be upon your faces that you do not sin.

21 And the people stood afar off, and Moses came near to the thick darkness there where God was."

This passage of scripture tells us that Israel was terrified upon hearing it. But in fact it offers a blessing, and a promise. Moses and the Prophets ensure that we sinners hear the law and the commandments as well as the good news that stops us from perishing in Hell.

As Jesus says to his disciples in Matt. 16:24-28; *"Then Jesus said to his disciples, If anyone wills to come after me, let him utterly deny himself, and lift up his cross, and follow me,*
25 Because whoever wills to save his soul will destroy it, and whoever will destroy his soul on account of me will find it;
26 Because what will a man be benefited, if he should gain the whole world, but experience the loss of his soul? Or what will a man give in exchange for his soul?
27 Because the Son of Man is about to come in the glory of his Father with his heavenly messengers, and then he will give back to everyone according to his action.
28 Amen, I say to you that, There are some standing here who will absolutely not taste of death until they see the Son of Man coming in his kingdom."

In both the law and gospel, God proclaims His work, and he demands that His people respond by obeying his commands. The terms "law" and "Gospel" differ in emphasis, as they overlap and intertwine. They permit to show the Word of God is from different perspectives.

Therefore we can conclude by saying that the Bible is both law (because as a whole it speaks with divine authority and requires belief) and Gospel (because it is good news to fallen creatures). Each concept is meaningless without the other.

The law often brings terror. Israel was frightened by the wrath of God against their sin on Mount Sinai.

Ex. 20:18-21; *"And all the people saw the voices, and the flames, and the voice of the trumpet, and the mountain smoking; and when the people saw, they vacillated back and forth, and stood afar off.*
19 And they said to Moses, You speak with us, and we will attentively hear; and do not let God speak with us lest we die.
20 And Moses said to the people; Do not fear, because God has come in order to test you, and that his fear may be upon your faces that you do not sin.
21 And the people stood afar off, and Moses came near to the thick darkness there where God was."

But it also brings delight to the redeemed heart.

Psalm. 1:2; *"But his delight is in the law of Jehovah, and in his law he murmurs in pleasure day and night."*

Rom. 7:22; *"Because I delight in the law of God according to the inward man."*

The Gospel brings comfort and joy; but it also brings condemnation. Paul says that his preaching of the Gospel is to those who have already perished, "a fragrance from death to death" and, to those who believe, "a fragrance from life to life"

2 Cor. 2:15-16; *"Because we are a good smell of Christ to God in those being saved, and in those being destroyed; To the one the smell of death into death, and to the others the smell of life into life, and who is sufficient for these things?"*

2 Cor. 4:3-4; *"And if truly our good news is hid, it is hid to them who are being destroyed, In whom the god of this age has blinded the exercising of the minds of the unbelieving, lest the light of the glorious good news of Christ, who is the image of God, should shine to them."*

Rom. 9:32; *"Why? Because it was absolutely not out of faith but in the manner of law works, because they stumbled at the Stone of Stumbling;"*

The Gospel is good news to all those who believe. But for those amongst us who are intent on saving themselves by their own righteousness, it is not good news at all. It is God's condemnation upon them that becomes their own rock of offense.

Which Comes First the Law or the Gospel?

It is the law first and the Gospel second. We are told that people must be scared of the law before they can be driven to seek salvation in Christ. Despite there being a great need to preach God's standards, man's disobedience, and God's wrath against sin, especially in an age such as ours where people think God will let them behave as they like. Yet it is by the conviction of the Holy Spirit that people have been driven to their knees in repentance when the Spirit has convicted them of their transgressions of the law.

However, it is really impossible to present law without gospel or gospel without law, though various relative emphases are possible. God declares that he has redeemed his people (gospel), and then asks them to behave as his covenant people (law). Since both gospel and law are aspects of God's covenants, that pattern is heard and spoken of through the word of God himself in the Bible.

Jesus reflects this in his own evangelism. For in the chapter of John 4, Jesus tells the Samaritan woman that he can give her living water that will take away all thirst. Only after offering that gift of water does Jesus proclaim the law to her, exposing her adultery.

In Luke 18:18—30 Jesus says; *"And a certain ruler asked him, saying, inherently Good Teacher, what shall I do to inherit eternal life?*
19 And Jesus said to him, Why do you say to me, inherently Good? Absolutely not one is inherently good, except one, God.
20 You see the commandments, Do not commit adultery. Do not murder. Do not steal. Do not bear false witness. Honour your father and mother.
21 And he said, I have kept all these from my youth.
22 And Jesus hearing these things, said to him, Yet one commandment to you is lacking; sell all, as much as you have, and distribute to the poor, and you will have treasure in heaven, and come here; follow me.
23 And hearing these things, he became intensely sad, because he was exceedingly rich.
24 And Jesus seeing him become intensely sad, said, With difficulty will those having riches enter into the kingdom of God,
25 Because it is easier for a camel to enter through the eye of a needle, than for one rich to enter into the kingdom of God.
26 And those hearing it said, And who has the power to be saved?
27 And he said, The things impossible with men are possible with God.
28 Then Peter said, Behold, we have left all, and followed you.
29 And he said to them, Amen I say to you, There is absolutely not one who has left house, or parents, or brothers, or Pharisee and the tax collector; let the children come; a rich ruler; A camel ...the eye of a needle wife, or children, for the sake of the kingdom of God,
30 Who shall not receive many times more in this present time, and in the coming age life

everlasting."

In this passage we can see that Jesus does not use the law alone to terrorize man or to plunge him into despair. The man does go away only after Jesus had called him to discipleship, which, though itself is a command, it is the command of the Gospel.

What are the "New Perspectives" and Paul's Gospel?

The apostle Paul is deemed by many as showing us through the gospel and his writings the fulfilment of God's promise to Abraham to bless all nations.

The "works of the law" which Paul highlights are not merely man's attempts to satisfy God's moral law, but the distinctions between Jews and Gentiles such as circumcision, food laws, and cleansings.

Rom. 4:4-5; *"And to the one working, the pay is absolutely not calculated according to grace, but according to what is owed. And to him not working, but believing upon the one who justifies the ungodly; his faith is calculated for righteousness."*

Rom. 11:6; *"And if by grace, it is absolutely no longer out of works, otherwise grace is absolutely no longer grace, and if out of works, it is absolutely no longer grace, otherwise work is absolutely no longer work."*

Eph. 2:8-10; *"Because by grace you are saved, through faith, and that absolutely not out of yourselves; it is the gift of God,*

9 Absolutely not out of works, so that no one should boast, 10 Because we are his workmanship, created in Christ Jesus upon inherent good works, which God has prepared beforehand so that we should walk in them."

Phil. 3:9; *"And be found in him, not having my righteousness, the one out of the law, but the one through Christ's faith, the out of God righteousness upon the faith."*

These scriptures show us clearly that Paul rejects, not only legal barriers between Jew and Gentile, but he also informs us of all attempts people go to, too save themselves by their works.

Yet there are many that have come to think of the Gospel as correlative with faith and law as correlative with works. We need to understand that it is the, law that condemns and the Gospel that saves.

What are the Law and Gospel and the Christian Life?

The answer can be found in the bible. When Scripture presents us with a command, we need to be obedient to that command. This is a righteous action, as our righteousness is measured by our obedience to God's commands.

When God threatens punishment upon us, and we turn from this wickedness to do what God asks, this is not a sin, but a righteous response. When God promises to reward us and bless us, it is a good thing for us to embrace that reward and blessing.

There are many Christians who do not follow what is written in the word and are thus classed as carnal Christians, as they conduct their lives completely apart from the admonitions of God's word.

They ignore God's revelation of his righteousness is, which is essentially sinful. They read the Scripture, but refuse to follow its commands to change one's conduct, and as a result that is the essence of sin.

Therefore to conclude we are to follow the commands and be obedient to the word of God.

Law of God

The following extract is taken from the Westminster Confession of Faith XIX where it tells us;

I. God gave to Adam a law, as a covenant of works, by which he bound him and all his posterity to personal, entire, exact, and perpetual obedience, promised life upon the fulfilling, and threatened death upon the breach of it, and endued him with power and ability to keep it.

II. This law, after his fall, continued to be a perfect rule of righteousness; and, as such, was delivered by God upon Mount Sinai, in ten commandments, and written in two tables: the first four commandments containing our duty towards God; and the other six, our duty to man.

III. Beside this law, commonly called moral, God was pleased to give to the people of Israel, as a church under age, ceremonial laws, containing several typical ordinances, partly of worship, prefiguring Christ, his graces, actions, sufferings, and benefits; and partly, holding forth divers instructions of moral duties. All which ceremonial laws are now abrogated, under the New Testament.

IV. To them also, as a body politic, he gave sundry judicial laws, which expired together with the State of that people; not obliging any other now, further than the general equity thereof may require.

V. The moral law doth forever bind all, as well justified persons as others, to the obedience thereof; and that, not only in regard of the matter contained in it, but also in respect of the authority of God the Creator, who gave it. Neither doth Christ, in the gospel, any way dissolve, but much strengthens this obligation.

VI. Although true believers be not under the law, as a covenant of works, to be thereby justified, or condemned; yet is it of great use to them, as well as to others; in that, as a rule of life informing them of the will of God, and their duty, it directs and binds them to walk accordingly; discovering also the sinful pollutions of their nature, hearts, and lives; so as, examining themselves thereby, they may come to further conviction of, humiliation for, and hatred against sin, together with a clearer sight of the need they have of Christ, and the perfection of his obedience. It is likewise of use to the regenerate, to restrain their corruptions, in that it forbids sin: and the threatenings of it serve to show what even their sins deserve; and what afflictions, in this life, they may expect for them, although freed from the curse thereof threatened in the law. The promises of it, in like manner, show them God's approbation of obedience, and what blessings they may expect upon the performance thereof: although not as due to them by the law as a covenant of works. So as, a man's doing good, and refraining from evil, because the law encourageth to the one, and deterreth from the other, is no evidence of his being under the law; and, not under grace.

VII. Neither are the fore mentioned uses of the law contrary to the grace of the gospel, but do sweetly comply with it; the Spirit of Christ subduing and enabling the will of man to do that freely, and cheerfully, which the will of God, revealed in the law, requireth to be done.

Therefore to understand this fully we need to understand the nature of the law.

What is the Nature of Law?

To fully understand the law we must begin with a right understanding of the infinite, eternal and unchangeable God. His nature, unlike our own, doesn't depend on things outside of Himself.

God is independent. This is evident from His own revelation which is shown to us in the Scripture. Only He alone is eternal, and He is the origin of all things, which outside of Him, has never changed throughout time.

God is complete in Himself, His knowledge and His decrees. God confirms the unity of His being through the Scriptures.

God's attributes are separated only in their revelation to us by which we cannot comprehend as His nature is whole. In God there is His mercy which is different from the doctrines of justice, holiness, eternality, truth and the other characteristics of the godhead.

When we study the Bible, God wrote it not just for our information which is organized into categories that can be labelled and fitted together into a system. But He wrote it in a way that our infinite minds can handle masses of data to be able to simplify the concepts that were written. And that our study agrees with what God has written about himself in the Bible, and that our understanding corresponds with the whole truth in which the Eternal Lord knows it.

Law is a concept which we tend to isolate and then examine as if it had an existence of its own. As individuals we tend to think of our own individual precepts that bind us morally or civilly.

However, law has its origin in the unified and independent nature of God. What God is pleased about is that which is consistent with His purpose. As our Creator this by definition is moral and right.

God alone is eternal, there was a moment in time, before nothing else but God existed. No other beings existed so there was no sin except by definition.

As there was no one to whom God could communicate His truth and glory too, there wasn't to be the need of His revelation. Since there was no need for boundaries to be set either for others to understand what pleases God, there was no need for the law.

Yet in the eternal mind of God, His moral principles persisted without any change. These moral principles had always and will always exist forever in the godhead. As they provide us with the only foundation for the idea of law.

What is meant by the Place of Law in God's Creation?

Genesis 1: 1-2 says; *"First God created the heavens and the earth. And the earth was lying waste and empty, and darkness was upon the face of the deep. And the Spirit of God brooded upon the face of the waters."*

The word created, in Hebrew is Bara, which means to bring into existence by cutting it out, as a tailor cuts out a garment.

Therefore, everything in the material world was not created from nothing, but God used words to cut matter out of the spiritual reality in Himself. The word Bara occurs 57 times in the Bible and every place would make good sense if we translated it cut out (or down, etc.).

Gen 1:1 as translated, First God cut out the heavens and the earth...God cut the material, psychological (soulical, animal, and human), and the human spirits out of the spiritual reality within Himself.

It is used at three strategic places in Genesis 1.

In v. 1 **God created matter**, then made various parts of the universe from that matter.
In v. 21 **God created soul life**, and made various types of living creatures from that soul life.
In v. 27 **God created spirit life** in Adam (and separated Eve from Adam), and from those two all humans have been made, with a spirit in the likeness of God, with a soul in common with animals, and with a body in common with the earth.

In all the other verses the word made is used, Hebrew, asah. It means to make from existing materials. God created all things by His Spirit from within Himself by means of words.

His words are spirit and life, John 6:63; *"The Spirit is the one who makes alive; the flesh benefits absolutely not one thing; the spoken words that I speak to you are spirit, and they are life."*

They were the force by which spiritual reality was projected from inside of God into material reality. His words were the tools by which He cut out and created and made all things.

We do not "create" anything in the ultimate meaning of that word, but we call things that are not in our lives from God's treasures, as though they were, and they are to us through faith, Rom 4:17; *"As it has been written, I have placed you a father of many races, before God whom he believed, who makes the dead alive, and calls the things not being as being,"*

The word heavens, in Hebrew is shamayim, it is always plural, meaning:
1. The atmosphere around the earth.
2. The heavenly space where the other planets and stars are.
3. The third heaven where God's throne is.

2 Cor. 12:2; *"I saw a man in Christ fourteen years before – whether in body, I absolutely did not see, or outside the body, I absolutely did not see; God saw - that such a one was caught up to the third heaven."*

Psalm 68:33; *"To him who rides upon the heavens of heavens of old; lo, he gives his voice, a mighty voice."*

Psalm 148:4; *"Boast in him, Oh heavens of the heavens, and you waters which are above the heavens."*

God's dwelling place is in all three,

1 Kings 8:30; *"And you attentively hear the stooping down for grace of your servant, and of your people Israel, when they shall judge in prayer toward this place, and attentively hear in the heavens, your dwelling place; and when you attentively hear, forgive."*

Although all the heavens cannot contain Him,

1 Kings 8:27; *"Because, will God truly dwell on the earth? Behold, the heavens and the heaven of heavens cannot contain you, how much less this house that I have built?"*

The earth, is the only place in the universe where plant, animal, and human life have ever existed, or will ever exist until the New Heaven and New Earth. No other heavenly body has the proper conditions to sustain earthly life.

Ps 115:16; *"The heavens - the heavens are Jehovah's, and he has given the earth to the children of Adam."*

We can see that God made it that way. Everything God the Father does is through God the Son, Jesus Christ, and by the power of God the Holy Spirit.

John 1:3; *"All things were caused to be through him, and apart from him absolutely not one thing was caused to be that was caused to be."*

Heb 9:14; *"How much more will the blood of Christ, who through the eternal Spirit offered himself unblemished to God, cleanse your conscience from dead works for ministering to the living God?"*

The Spirit of God had managed to push and pull everything into its form and place. When God created the universe, regardless of our levels of understanding, the infinite began to make itself known in the finite.

Then when God created animals and humans, moral law then appeared as part of the Creator's handiwork, this reflecting on His eternal and indivisible nature.

The purpose of creation is made clear in the Bible as declaring the glory and nature of God:

Psalm 19:1 *"The heavens are telling the glory of God; and the firmament is declaring the work of His hands."*

Romans 1:20 *"For since the creation of the world His invisible attributes, His eternal power and divine nature, have been clearly seen, being understood through what has been made, so that they are without excuse."*

From the moment moral beings came into existence, it is right that they should have and honour no other gods than the one who made them for His own glory. The spirit nature of God, being revealed in what was made. This should never to be confused by making physical images of Him.

The name of God is to be guarded against being used in vain.

The first three examples of moral law in the Ten Commandments are not temporal rules. These rules flow from the very nature of God Himself and are based upon eternal and unchangeable principles.

Now with the completion of the creation, God ceased bringing new things into being and commanded that the Sabbath Day be sanctified to remember his work. This is because all things were made to reveal his divine glory; it would be immoral for any being not to respond to that revealed glory of worship in which God reveals how He is to be worshipped.

Therefore the Sabbath law proceeds from the very nature of the Creator as He relates it to His creation.

When man was created there had to be rules made to preserve the mark of the eternal Artist on his handiwork. God told him that he must work. Man's role was to exercise his appointed and representative dominion over the rest of creation.

God commanded that the one man and one woman who He had created should become one flesh in a convent union to produce children and populate His world. These precepts were not temporal, but flowed from the eternal nature and plan of God himself as Creator of all things.

Up to this point mankind had not fallen into sin.

What is meant by Covenant of Works?

The covenant of works is when the Sovereignty of God is revealed in his promises to Adam. Adam was the one appointed to represent all of His prosperity descended from him by natural generation. As the nature of creature proceeds from the nature of God. This is His purpose in creation; the obedience has to be complete and individual. Adam was bound by various creational ordinances which were revealed to him by God.

This included the strict observance of the Sabbath Day. Including the six days of faithful labour which was to exercise dominion over creation, fidelity to his wife and the producing godly offspring to fill the earth.

We can see this in Genesis 2:1-9; *"earth were finished, and all the hosts of them.*
2 And on the seventh day God finished his work which he had made, and he rested on the seventh day from all his work which he had made.
3 And God blessed the seventh day, and sanctified it, because that in it he rested from all his work which God had created to make.
4 These are the generations of the heavens and of the earth when they were created, in the day of Jehovah God's making the earth and the heavens,
5 And every shrub of the field before it was in the earth, and every plant of the field before it sprouted, because Jehovah God had not caused it to rain on the earth and Adam did not exist to work the soil.
6 And a mist ascended out of the earth, and watered all the face of the soil.
7 And Jehovah God formed the man out of the dust of the soil, and breathed into his nostrils the breath of life; and the man became a living soul.
8 And Jehovah God planted a garden in Eden in the east, and put there the man whom he had formed.
9 And out of the soil Jehovah God sprouted every tree delightful to the sight, and good for food, and the tree of life in the midst of the garden, and the tree of the knowledge of good and evil."

We can also see that Adam was commanded to abstain from eating the fruit of the tree of the knowledge of good and evil. God promised life to Adam if he obeyed; and threatened death if he transgressed.

These elements confirmed the use of the term covenant in describing this relationship. This is what is deemed as the Covenant of Works.

The duty imposed upon Adam was beyond his own capacity particularly in his original created state. As we can see in the events that followed, he had the ability to disobey God.

Genesis 3:6-24; *"And because the woman saw the tree good for food, and because she saw it as a delight to the eyes, and a tree craved to make one intelligently successful, she took from its fruit, and ate, and gave also to her mortal man with her; and he ate.*
7 And the eyes of them both were opened, and they knew by seeing that they were naked; and they sewed fig leaves together, and made themselves girdles.
8 And they attentively heard the voice of Jehovah God walking in the garden in the Spirit of the day, and the man and his wife hid themselves from the face of Jehovah God among the trees of the

garden.
9 And Jehovah God called to the man, and said to him, Where are you?
10 And he said, I attentively heard your voice in the garden, and I was afraid, because I was naked; and I hid myself.
11 And he said, Who caused it to stand out boldly to you that you were naked? Have you eaten of the tree, of which I commanded you that you should not eat?
12 And the man said, The woman whom you gave to be with me, she gave me from the tree, and I ate.
13 And Jehovah God said to the woman, What is this that you have done? And the woman said, The snake deceived me, and I ate.
14 And Jehovah God said to the snake, Because you have done this, you are cursed above all living things, and above all animals of the field; you shall walk on your belly, and you shall eat dust all the days of your life;
15 And I will put hostility between you and the woman, and between your seed and her seed; he shall overwhelm your head, and you shall overwhelm his heel.
16 He said to the woman, Multiplying, I will multiply your painful labour and your conception; you shall bear children in painful labour; and your longing shall be to your husband, and he shall rule over you.
17 And he said to Adam, Because you have heard attentively the voice of your wife, and have eaten of the tree, of which I commanded you, saying, You shall not eat of it, the soil is cursed because of you; you shall eat of it all the days of your life in painful labour;
18 And it shall sprout thorns and thistles to you and you shall eat the plants of the field;
19 You shall eat food in the sweat of your nostrils until you turn back to the soil, because you have been taken out of it, because you are dust, and you shall turn back to dust.
20 And the man called his wife's name Eve, because she became the mother of all living.
21 And Jehovah God made for the man and his wife coats of skins, and clothed them.
22 And Jehovah God said, Behold, the man has become as one of us, to know by seeing good and evil; and now, so that he does not send out his hand, and take also of the tree of life, and eat, and live forever,
23 Jehovah God sent him out of the Garden of Eden to work the soil, there from where he was taken.
24 And he drove the man out, and he lodged the Cherubs on the east of the Garden of Eden, and a blazing sword turning every way to hedge about the way of the tree of life."

It is the sin of Adam where we see the greater plan of God. God created man as finite, mutable, and a fallible creature. The notion behind the principle of federal headship which treats mankind representatively, not only in the fall, is also found in the redemption by Jesus Christ in the Covenant of Grace.

What is the Law after the fall of Man?

The sin of Adam corrupted all of mankind. God had to make known His precepts. He did this much later where the Creator Himself gave them to Moses on Mt. Sinai.

These are the Ten Commandments, yet according to many they did not originate any new moral principles. They state in summary form the moral principle that prevails in God's creation so that it reflects the glory of His Holiness.

Moral principles derive from the nature of the Creator. It is not possible for these principles to be classed as unimportant or optional in a creation that is originally intended to declare the Creator's glory, eternal power and divine nature.

The very nature of God is eternal and unchangeable, so must the moral principles of his creation be continuously abiding and unchangeable.

God had made all of His Creation to declare His glory; this includes his holiness and justice. God also makes known his moral principles by demanding all moral creatures to obey them perfectly and personally.

We are to honour God, and to live at peace with his creation (including other humans) requires that the revealed moral law should be obeyed.

The Ten Commandments

Exodus 20:3-17; *"There shall not be to you any other gods before my face.*
4 You shall not make for yourselves carved idols, or any likeness that is in the heavens above, or that is in the earth beneath, or that is in the water under the earth;
5 You shall not prostrate yourself to them, and you shall not serve them, because I, Jehovah, your God, am a jealous God, visiting the iniquity of the fathers upon the children to the third and fourth generation of them who hate me;
6 And doing mercy to thousands of them who love me, and hedge about my commandments.
7 You shall not lift the name of Jehovah, your God, for ruin, because Jehovah will not consider him clean who lifts his name for ruin.
8 Remember the Sabbath day to keep it holy.
9 You shall work six days, and do all your work;
10 And the seventh day is the Sabbath of Jehovah, your God; you shall not do any work, you, or your son, or your daughter, your manservant, or your maidservant, or your animals, or your stranger who is within your gates,
11 Because Jehovah made the heavens and earth, the sea, and all that is in them in six days, and rested the seventh day; therefore Jehovah blessed the Sabbath day, and sanctified it.
12 Heavily honour your father and your mother, so that your days may be long upon the soil which Jehovah, your God, gives you.
13 You shall not kill.
14 You shall not commit adultery.
15 You shall not steal.
16 You shall not answer false testimony against your neighbour.
17 You shall not covet your neighbour's house; you shall not covet your neighbour's wife, or his manservant, or his maidservant, or his ox, or his donkey, or anything that is your neighbour's."

And repeated in Deuteronomy 5:7-21; *"There shall not be other gods to you before my face.*
8 You shall not make for yourself any carved image, any likeness of what is in the heavens above, or what is in the earth beneath, or what is in the waters beneath the earth.
9 You shall not prostrate yourself to them, and you shall not serve them, because I Jehovah, your God, am a jealous God, visiting the iniquity of the fathers on the children, and on the third and fourth generation of those hating me,
10 And doing mercy to thousands of them who love me and hedge about my commandments.
11 You shall not take up the name of Jehovah, your God, for ruin, because Jehovah will not hold him to be clean who takes up his name for ruin.
12 Hedge about the Sabbath day to sanctify it, what Jehovah, your God, commanded you.
13 You shall work six days, and do all your work,
14 And the seventh day is the Sabbath of Jehovah, your God; you shall not do any work, you, nor your son, nor your daughter, nor your male servant, nor your female servant, nor your ox, nor your donkey, nor any of your animals, nor your guest who is within your gates, so that your male servant and your female servant may rest as you.
15 And remember that you were a servant in the land of Egypt, and that Jehovah, your God, brought you out from there through a strong hand, and by a stretched out arm; therefore Jehovah, your God, commanded you to hedge about the Sabbath day.
16 Heavily honour your father and your mother, what Jehovah, your God, commanded you, so that your days may be long, and that it may be well with you, in the land which Jehovah, your God, gives you.
17 You shall not kill.
18 You shall not commit adultery.
19 You shall not steal.

20 You shall not respond with ruinous testimony against your neighbour.
21 You shall not covet your neighbour's wife, and you shall not covet your neighbour's house, his field, or his male servant, or his female servant, his ox, or his donkey, or anything that is your neighbour's."

The Ten Commandments are the moral principles in the eternal nature of God himself; their violation is a crime against the purpose of the universe which is to glorify God.

When challenged, Jesus further summarized the law in two statements. He used the words of Moses to show that this was not a new concept but had already been clearly revealed.

His answer to his critics came from Deuteronomy 6:5; *"And you shall love Jehovah, your God, with all your heart, and with all your soul, and with all your might."*

Leviticus 19:18; *"You shall not avenge nor cherish a grudge against the children of your people, but you shall love your neighbour as yourself; I am Jehovah."*

Matthew 22:37-40 *"And He said to him, 'You shall love the Lord your God with all your heart, and with all your soul, and with your entire mind. This is the great and foremost commandment. And a second is like it, You shall love your neighbour as yourself. On these two commandments depend the whole law and the prophets."*

The first four commandments show our creaturely obligations towards God. They are reflected in Jesus summary from Deuteronomy 6:5 *"And you shall love Jehovah, your God, with all your heart, and with all your soul, and with all your might."*

The last six commandments show our obligations towards one another as God's creatures.

They are summarized as Jesus quotes from Leviticus 19:18 *"You shall not avenge nor cherish a grudge against the children of your people, but you shall love your neighbour as yourself; I am Jehovah."*

In our modern society, where the God of the Bible is denied and his law is despised, the moral principles are inverted. The following shows how the Ten Commandments represent the moral values that are growing in today's culture:

1. Society worships more than one God.

2. They do not believe the physical universe is real.

3. The name of God is no longer honoured as blasphemy and crude language have become the accepted idiom...

4. The Sabbath has become a day for man and not for God as the Sabbath becomes a prime day for commerce, particularly in support of restaurants, special sales of merchandise, professional sports, and entertainment.

5. People have a lack of respect and regard of authority as children become answerable to the state and society rather than to parents.

6. Human life is only honoured when it serves a person's interests as the unborn are put to death and capital criminals are set free.

7. Sexual freedom is no longer regulated as marriage has become option and divorce has become an easy answer to abandon oaths and vows.

8. Theft has become an acceptable tolerance in today's society and also the state, not the individual, controls the rightful distribution of wealth and ownership.

9. Truth is now difficult to define as lies are seen as the truth, even when the truth when told provides one with an unpleasant outcome.

10. Coveting is now deemed as good for personal growth and advancement, as self-esteem has become the highest good. Aggressiveness and greed are the most prized attributes in our economy and culture.

These commandments are seen to relate to today's society and are better known as the devils plan. The devil doesn't want us to be obedient to God; he doesn't want us to receive the gift of live through asking God for repentance and forgiveness. He wants us to all perish and go to hell.

But the bible clearly states the Laws, in which we are to follow,

1. One True and only God

When God spoke to Moses...*Thou shalt have no other Gods before me.* God could see clearly how the Devil would persuade and tempt people away from this law, as in Matthew 4:10 it is written again (KJV)...*Thou shalt worship the Lord thy God and him only shalt thou serve.*

The Devil continues to manipulate and turn people away from worshipping God, and from believing in Lord Jesus Christ, its happening around us.

If you asked your friend, do you believe in Lord Jesus Christ?

They would answer yeah an old figure from history.

The Devil blinds people from accepting God's word; he cleverly tempts them away from truly believing along with his gang of demons.

There are people that are so wealthy that they love money more than God. And there are those that are so poor they are being blinded from accepting God's love and his hand. They stubbornly refuse to turn to him and ask God for help. Because the Devils gang of fallen angels ensures they continue to live in misery.

The world politicians do not want us to worship God in the way that God wants. Some politicians even think they are God by making false promises that never come to fruition when they are elected.

One such politician remaining nameless promised on improving education with the slogan Education, Education, Education. But the reality sadly is the standards of education have fallen and religious instruction is falling as well in all private and public sector schools.

Gone are the days where songs were sung in assembly to worship God, and only the bible was taught in schools with teachings on how to pray and to accept Jesus God's only son and saviour.

If schools continued to do this, then the politically correct and heretic people would take offense as it is not allowing our children to learn about other religions.

Therefore worshipping God and only God and the true Gospel has been taken out of our institutions.

Thus resulting in only victory for the heretics and those who choose to be the followers of Satan. This is what Satan wants to turn children away from God and become a worshipper of false gods, toys and money rather than taught to worship God and his word.

The effects of these heretics is now being felt across society as more and more people turn away from the truth...

1Timothy 6:5 ; *"Perverse disputing's of men of corrupt minds, and destitute of the truth, supposing that gain is godliness: from such withdraw thyself."*

But those of us who worship God and only God have been shown in 1 Thessalonians 5:2-3; *"For yourselves know perfectly that the day of the Lord so cometh as a thief in the night. For when they shall say, peace and safety; then sudden destruction cometh upon them, as travail upon a woman with child; and they shall not escape."*

In other words those people who continue to worship other Gods, God will destroy. Yet when that time comes we are who truly believe and worship God only and believe that his son Jesus Christ at his baptism had all our sins where placed upon him then crucified for them, will be saved and protected from the destruction which is soon to befall upon the earth.

2. Idolistic and Material world

Spring is one of the most glorious seasons of the year; it is this season which reminds me of how God really takes living things from looking like they are dead to becoming alive with colour, radiance and full of bloom. But sadly as time goes by, people are no longer look at this season and thank the Lord for all his glory. Their eyes and minds have become closed to this.

As God says to Moses...

Thou shalt not make unto thee any craven image, or any likeness of anything that is in heaven above, or that is in the earth beneath, or that is in the water under the earth: Thou shalt not bow down thyself to them, nor serve them: For I the Lord thy God am a jealous God, visiting the iniquity of the fathers upon the children unto the third and fourth generation of them that hate me; and shewing mercy unto thousands of them that love me, and keep my commandments.

God also reiterates this statement both in 1 John 5:21, and Acts 17:29...

Little children, keep yourselves from idols. For as much then as we are the offspring of God, we ought not to think that the God head is like unto gold or silver, or stone, graven by art and man's device.

How many of you as children fell fowl to following your favourite band or artist?

I can tell you that there isn't a person on this earth that has not ever done that. It may not necessarily be an artist in a form of a musician, it could be an actress or even everyday things like cars, computers, houses or buying the latest technology, or looking at someone wishing you could be like them.

In other words loving material things and people more than God. Some Christians would say I love God he is my idol. Jesus is my saviour, yet they also have the love of money and what money can buy. They would rather be rich than poor. So how can they be deemed as saying I love God and only God; and all that God is?

Yet in their prays, I must have that house, I must have that car, I must buy that latest gadget. I must be better and more powerful than thy neighbour.

Excuse me, hang on.

These people on Sunday will praise the Lord, preach the gospel, and say thank you for saving my life Jesus, I love you, oh Lord. But in their hearts I have knew the truth is written.

A man who has nothing who comes to believe and accept Jesus as his or her saviour truly loves God and everything he stands for and worships only him. They see when they get a job a blessing not, I must get a job to have a nice holiday, a luxury car, get a handful of doe to give to the church, because they feel that by giving on Sunday it will ease them. And release them from the guilt of not worshipping God and only God 100% and putting him and his son Jesus above all other things.

When non believers read and see how wealthy these men and women of God as some of them profess to be are, it puts them off. They tell me how can we accept Jesus as our Lord and saviour and believe in him when the so called me of God, all they can address is money in their sermons and worldly things, professing the word of the Lord by saying give totally one self into Jesus, believe in him and he will reward you with riches.

They forget the point riches means eternal life, they make it known as riches being, a better paid job, a bigger car etc.

And when these things do not materialise then people become disillusioned and turn away from God. It just makes me so sick, that I didn't become a born again Christian to be better off in this world. I became born again to live my live like Jesus did without fault and love for all things God created not those in which man has created.

As Jesus tells us in John 14:1-2 KJV...

Let not your heart be troubled: ye believe in God, believe also in me. In my father's house are many mansions: if it were not so, I would have told you. I go to prepare a place for you.

Jesus is not talking about a mansion on earth, but a mansion that God has built in heaven for all that receive him. By receiving is accepting and becoming like Jesus.

Jesus never profited on earth, as he says in John 12:49-50; *"For I have not spoken of myself; but the father which sent me, he gave me a commandment, what I should say, and what I should speak. And I know that his commandment is life everlasting: what so ever I speak therefore, even as the father said unto me, so I speak."*

Jesus knows that all of us humans who speak of him and the Lord God but do not profit from this, will have everlasting life. What I mean by profiting is becoming rich on earth, loving the worldly things that man has made rather than that of God and God's creation.

As Paul went and preached the gospel the true word of God, he told the crowd of people who gathered at Mars hill in Athens...

Acts 17:22-24; *"Ye men of Athens I perceive that in all things ye are too superstitious. For as I passed by, and beheld your devotions I found an alter with this inscription, TO THE UNKNOWN GOD. Whom therefore ye ignorantly worship, him declare I unto you. God made the world and all things therein, seeing that he is Lord of heaven and earth, dwelleth not in temples made with hands."*

Therefore if one does all these things that have been mentioned then he has just fallen fowl of God, but living with the Devil and his followers. Who as told throughout the Bible can pose as an angel of light, preaching false doctrine, and earning big sums of money in the process; in order to tempt people away from following and worshipping God our creator of all living things.

In 1 Thessalonians 4:14-18; *"For if we believe that Jesus died and rose again, even so them also which sleep in Jesus will God bring with him. For this we say unto you by the word of the Lord, that we which are alive and remain unto the coming of the Lord shall not prevent them which are asleep. For the Lord himself shall descent from heaven with a shout, with the voice of the archangel, and with the trump of God: and the dead in Christ shall rise first: Then we which are alive and remain shall be caught up together with them in the clouds to meet the Lord in the air: and so shall we ever be with the Lord. Wherefore comfort one another with these words."*

3. Blasphemy

The glory of God can be felt today as the heat of the sun comes down with a smile. Yet people will not look upon this as a blessing from God, but look to the sun's heat and say...'J thanks God I can have a great tan now', and then wonder why they are burnt by the sun.

As God says first to Moses...

Thou shalt not take the name of the Lord thy God in vain; for the Lord will not hold him guiltless that taketh his name in vain.

And again it is recorded in 1 Timothy 6:1; *"That the name of God and his doctrine be not blasphemed."*

Therefore in the sentence 'Gee thanks God I can have a great tan now.' This is seen as using God's name in vain, and this is happening everyday.

People blame God for all the troubles in their lives. They cry out Why God, Why have you done this? Not asking him truly, sincerely and faithfully for the Lord to reply to discipline and to help you in your walk with me.

But they ask God with anger and full of bitterness. Not in love, and for this God does not reply. But only the Devil and his demon followers who tempt these people continuously away from God cause more pain and suffering.

The evidence speaks for itself in both the world and in the personal lives of the unsaved. It is not God that causes this but man's continual defiance to turn to him and accept the truth. Hence why they blaspheme and use his name in vain, because this is what the Devil wants.

4. The Sabbath

From the beginning of time God asks just one thing of us, and that is...*Remember the Sabbath day, to keep it holy. Six days shalt thou labour, and do all thy work; but the seventh day is the Sabbath of the Lord thy God: in it thou shalt not do any work, thou, nor thy son, nor thy daughter, nor thy manservant, nor thy maidservant, nor thy cattle, nor thy stranger that is within thy gates: for in six days the Lord made heaven and earth, the sea, and all that, in them is, and rested the seventh day: wherefore the Lord blessed the Sabbath day and hallowed it.*

And again this is reiterated throughout the New Testament, in Matthew 24:20 Mark 2:27-28, Hebrews 4:4, 9-10, and Colossians 1:16; *"Pray ye that your flight be not in winter, neither on the Sabbath day. The Sabbath was made for man, and not man for the Sabbath: therefore the son of man is Lord also of the Sabbath. For he spake in a certain place of the seventh day on this wise, And God did rest the seventh day from all his works. There remaineth therefore a keeping of a Sabbath to the people of God. For he that is entered unto his rest, he also hath ceased from his own works, as God did from his. For by him were all things created, that are in heaven and that are in earth."*

However during the later part of the 20th century, the idea of keeping the Sunday a holy day, where by everything is closed seems now to be a distant memory.

The Devil wants us to go shopping on Sunday, large companies, big cooperation's want to continue operating on a Sunday. So they tempt the workers giving them more money to work on the day God has made holy.

The Devil doesn't want us to worship God and keep this day a holy day for him. The Devil wants to open the doors and allow man to continue his greed and materialistic ways of the world.

In some ways I am pleased that I live in France as the country in a small way still observes the Sabbath day as a holy day, ordered by the Pope in which the cardinals writes the following question and answer in their literature.

(Q) Have you any other ways of proving that the church has power to institute festivals of precept?
(A) Had she not such power...she could not have substituted the observance of Sunday, the first day of the week, for Saturday, the seventh day, a change for which there is no scriptural authority.

Yet despite this we are all breaking the law of God as we worship him on the first day Sunday and not the Saturday. This is classed as Heresy, precept upon precept.

Daniel 7:25; *"And he shall speak great words against the most high, and shall wear out the saints of the most high, and think to change times and laws: and they shall be given unto his hand until a time and times and the dividing of time."*

It is here that we can clearly see the Pope is the one Daniel is referring too. Who else has authority over all the catholic churches in Europe and the whole world?

It is the Pope.

Jesus warns us of false prophets and false witnesses, as in Matthew 24:11...

And many false prophets shall rise and deceive many.

The Catholic Church is one of many that Jesus makes reference too. It has a bible that is different from the holy bible which is the word of God. Jesus warns us again in, II Thessalonians 2:3-4...

And that man of sin be revealed, the son of perdition. Who opposeth and exalteth himself above all that is called God, or that is worshipped: So that he as God sitteth in the temple of God, shewing himself that he is God.

This is the clever work of the Devil, allowing a human being like you and I change the day of the Sabbath, to dictate the catholic way of life and even persecute those who do not obey. Because those who were persecuted know the truth as it is written in 1 Thessalonians 1:5-6...

For our Gospel came not unto you in word only, but also in power, and in much assurance; as ye know what manner of men we were among you for your sake. And ye became followers of us, and of the Lord, having received the word in much affliction with Joy of the Holy Ghost.

So who are you going to believe, a man who is like you and I of sin, heresy and lies, or the Gospel of truth and of the Holy Spirit that brings and fills our hearts with joy, peace and love for all that God is, and the things God created?

5. Honour

What a blessing it is to know that the Lord is there watching us, hearing us and walking with us every time we call onto him. God never lets us go. And for this we must give thanks and praise his name.

As to our own parents who brought us into this world in flesh, it is written...*Honour thy father and mother: that thy days may be long upon the land which the Lord they God giveth me.*

And again in Matthew 19:19...*Honour thy father and thy mother.*

How said it is too see that the new generation takes their parents for granted. They do not honour there fathers or mothers, or they do not honour neither parent.

In society where a large percentage of the populations are raised by single mothers and fathers is hard to believe. Children in those families just want, want, want and the parent gives into him or her, as they feel guilty if they do not.

But what the sad thing about this is the parents have lost control, the child no longer honours them, and never gives them a card or a present of thanks. They care too much for themselves than of their own mother and father.

Of course there are children born into this world who have lost either parents, or one parent through death. But there are a large percentage of children being cared for by one parent and step parents. Where honouring one's parents no longer matters as long as the child has everything he or she wants.

There is an unfortunate story of a child who was conceived not out of love, but as an object for money. The mother as soon as the child was born left the father; they were unmarried so divorce wasn't the problem. The mother raised that child alone and denied the father access, the child knew who the father was by name, denied him and only ever got in touch for MONEY.

Later it came to light the mother had many lovers, subjected her child to abuse, neglected her education. The child 16 years later taken into foster care does not know anything except what her mother taught, and those were respect and honour nothing.

This sad story breaks my heart to hear how children have become and becoming. One has to just look at the way children are in the streets, the way they talk to their parents. It is like they have been doctrine into evil, and see it as a way of life to have an evil heart.

The same can be said for many children in the Middle East who are seen as Martyrs if they attach a bomb to themselves and blow up non Islamic believers, thinking in the process they are honouring their mother and father in the name of Jihad.

Yet in Ephesians 6:1-2...

CHILDREN OBEY YOUR PARENTS IN THE LORD: FOR THIS IS RIGHT.
HONOUR THY FATHER AND MOTHER :(which is the first commandment with promise ;)

But however a large number of children in today's society are born out of all things contrary to what God wants, for it is written in Galatians 5:17-22...

For the flesh lusteth against the spirit, and the spirit against the flesh: and these are contrary the one to the other: so that ye cannot do the things that ye would.
But if ye be led of the spirit, ye are not under the law. Now the works of the flesh are manifest, which are these; Adultery, Fornication, Uncleanness, Lasciviousness, Idoltary, Witchcraft, Hatred, Variance, Emulations, Wrath, Strife, Sedition's, Heresies, Envyings, Murders, Drunkenness, Revellings, and such like: of the which I tell you before, as I have also told you in time past, that they which do such things shall not inherit the kingdom of God. But the fruit of the spirit is LOVE, JOY, PEACE, LONG SUFFERING, GENTLENESS, GOODNESS, and FAITH.

God wants us to love and honour our parents and one another. But those born out of God's plan which is LOVE, JOY, PEACE, LONG SUFFERING, GENTLENESS, GOODNESS, and FAITH are victims of the devil, and as a result will not inherit the kingdom of God.

As it is written in Galatians 6:6-8...

let him that is taught in the word communicate unto him that teacheth in all good things.
Be not deceived; God is not mocked: for what so ever a man soweth, that shall he also reap.
For he that soweth to his flesh, shall of the flesh reap corruption; but he that soweth to the spirit shall of the spirit reap life everlasting.

The longer I live to see how generation by generation falling away from the grace and love of God, and by denying his son Jesus. The more I see a world full of evil, a world where the good will be persecuted until the time of the end.

However Jesus has warned of this time in Matthew 23:33-39 KJV where we who are servants of God will be persecuted as it is written...

Ye serpents, ye generation of vipers, how can ye escape the damnation's of Hell? Wherefore, behold I send unto you prophets, and wise men, and scribes: and some of them ye shalt kill and crucify: and some of them ye shall scourge in your synagogues and persecute them from city to city.
That upon you may come all the righteous blood shed upon the earth, from the blood of Zach-a-rias, son of Bar-a-chias, whom ye slew between the temple and the alter.
Verily I say unto you, all these things shall come upon this generation.

O Jerusalem, Jerusalem, thou that killest the prophets, and stonest them which are sent unto thee, how often would I have gathered thy children together, even as a hen gathereth her chickens under her wings and ye would not!
Behold your house is left unto you desolate. For I say unto you. Ye shall not see me henceforth, till ye shall say Blessed is he that cometh in the name of the Lord.

What an honour it is to have one true God that so loves us that he sent his only son to save us so that we all have the opportunity to be saved and become like Jesus, one of his children.

6. Murders

Love is such a wonderful word. God loves us so much, but do we love God and others in the way God loves us?

The answer is sadly no. Only a very small percentage of the community or population LOVE God the way he loves us and fellow human beings in the same way God loves us.

However the bible points out where others are concerned... Thou shalt not kill. There are a vast majority of people who never murder anything except an ant, spider, etc.

But there is always a percentage that does kill another human being living amongst us in society. There are people that hate a human so much that they murder that person. It may be a stranger or someone they know.

Yet the bible says very clearly...Thou shalt not kill.

There is a subject which is accepted in today's society, but in the eyes of God it is murder. ABORTION is murder in God's eyes.

I am going to give you a testimony in which the Devil will be made know to you what his plan has been. The Devil and his demons hate us so much that allowing a man to violate a woman so that all she can do is abort the child, from always being tormented and reminded by the child of the sin that was committed is easier to abort it.

Then after the abortion the devil continues to torment you because you have sinned, committed murder got rid of one of God's creations.

In Ephesians 2:1-7...

And you hath he quickened, who were dead in trespasses and sins; Wherein in time past ye walked according to the course of this world, according to the prince of the power of the air, the spirit that now worketh in the children of disobedience:
Among whom also we all had our conversation in times past in the lusts of our flesh, fulfilling the desires of the flesh and of the mind; and were by nature the children of wrath, even as others.
But God, who is rich in mercy, for his great love wherewith he loved us, even when we were dead in sins hath quickened us together with Christ, (by grace ye are saved ;)
And hath raised us up together, and made us sit together in heavenly places in Christ Jesus:
That in the ages to come he might shew the exceeding riches of his grace and his kindness towards us through Christ Jesus.

But because God loves us so much, he is saying here OK you have may have killed or have anger on your heart but I forgive you, you are saved because you have repented of your sins and have accepted Jesus my son into your heart.

God has cast these demons away though his son Jesus Christ. We can no longer allow ourselves to be tormented by the devil.

The Devil's plan is two things:

1) To torment you in flesh and then in hell.
2) Give you all the idols and keep your eyes, mind and hearts closed from God's salvation and then torment you in hell.

The issue of abortion is still under much debate.

However with the prince of darkness largely in control of this world. As God tells us through his apostle Paul in 2 Corinthians 2:4-17...

For out of much affliction and anguish of heart I wrote unto you with many tears; not that ye should be grieved, but that ye might know the love which I have more abundantly unto you.
But if any have ceased grief, he hath no grieved me, but in part: that I may not overcharge you all.
Sufficient to such a man in this punishment, which was inflicted of many. So that the contrariwise ye ought rather to forgive him, and comfort him, lest perhaps such a one should be swallowed up with overmuch sorrow.
Wherefore I beseech you that ye would confirm your love toward him. For to this end also did I write, that I might know the proof of you whether ye be obedient in all things.
To whom ye forgive anything, I forgive also: for if I forgave anything, to whom I forgave it, for your sakes forgive I it in the person of Christ;
Lest Satan should get an advantage of us: for we are not ignorant of his devices.
Furthermore, when I came to Troas to preach Christ's gospel, and a door was opened unto me of the Lord, I had no rest in my spirit, because I found not Titus my brother: but taking my leave of them I went from thence into Macedonia.
Now thanks be unto God, which always causeth us to triumph in Christ, and maketh manifest the savour of his knowledge by us in every place.
For we are unto God a sweet savour of Christ, in them that are saved, and in them that perish:
To the one we are the savour of death unto death; and to the other the savour of life and life. And who is sufficient for these things?
For we are not as many, which corrupt the word of God: but as of sincerity, but as of God, in the sight of God speak we in Christ.

So even though Satan has his claws in every human as in nature we sin naturally. God has given us an opportunity to be saved through his son Jesus Christ. And to be broken free from the Devil's clutches.

Oh how Great God is praise be to his name our father and creator over everything. And to his only son Jesus who took on all our sins at his baptism and paid the price for them by being crucified on the cross.

Let's all rejoice and praise his name and sing songs of joy, and love as we are saved and are a child of God. Hallelujah.

7. Adultery

There are many gifts God gives each human being. One of these gifts is in the form of a marriage, a partnership with another human being as man, wife.

This is such a wonderful gift to have, as then a family is formed.

Sadly though in today's society man is not happy with marriage; they do not want to commit to a woman or woman does not want to commit to man, so they have many lovers.

The bible clearly states in both the Old and the New Testament...*Thou shalt not commit adultery.*

However a vast number of people do. There are more adulterers than those who are faithful to their wife or husband. Sex too many is like an idol, a drug. In today's world it is deemed bizarre if one has not had many lovers. Or one remains a virgin until the wedding.

The evidence in this is the high divorce rates we have in society. People have become selfish, they just think of themselves. They do not think of their husband or wife.
Nor do they think of their children. There are more and more children each year being born out of marriage who have many stepmothers or fathers in some cases.

So what is this saying to our children? What kind of education is this setting? In teen magazines it now talks openly about sex and sex related problems.

Children as young as 12 are having children. Marriage is no longer classed as a gift. Many people do not get married, but they have many children with different lovers.

However God's wrath will be felt on the day of judgement to the world as it is written in Proverbs 25: 4-5...

Take away thy dross from the silver, and there shall come forth a vessel for the finer.
Take away the wicked from before the king, and his throne shall be established in righteousness.

Fornicating with lots of partners is like adultery. It is abusing the body. Some people all they do is fornicate, they are not interested in marriage. There are others who live as man and wife but marriage is the last thing on their minds.

But when children are born, marriage has to be the answer. A happy family can be formed; marriage is a union binding of two people to form one. Both parents are important in raising a child and educating a child.

Family values are no longer a priority in a vast majority of people's minds as they just have sex for money and children as a commodity. A number of children are not born out of love but for money.

There are many fathers who are heartbroken by the actions of women who after the child is born leave the father and raise the child alone with many lovers.

So the question has to be asked, how is the child being educated if all he or she witnesses is adultery and fornication in the home?

Job 10: 18-22...

Wherefore then hast thou brought me forth out of the womb?
Oh that I had given up the ghost, and no eye had seen me!
I should have been as though I had not been; I should have been carried from the womb to the

grave.
Are not my days few? Cease then, and let me alone, that I may take comfort a little.
Before I go whence I shall not return, even to the land of darkness and the shadow of death; a land of darkness, as darkness itself; and of the shadows of death without any order, and where the light is as darkness.

What Job is making reference here is the condition of eternal life in Hell. If people do not open there eyes and stop the desire of using sex as an idol and begin to educate their children as God has instructed in the bible.

8. Thieves

The days are closing much quickly than ever before. Once the day seemed too long, now it seems to short. The reason for this is the age we live in.

There are more things to occupy us now like television, computers and game consoles. People are forgetting that God is control of the weather, the beauty that is surrounding us, and relationships with one another.

Instead people are relying too much on man made objects to keep them busy rather than spending quality time worshipping and studying the word of God as well as with one another. The more that new inventions come onto the market, the more we want it. But sometimes these things cost too much money, so many people resort to stealing.

God sees this as a sin, breaking both civil and God's law, as it is written clearly in both the Old and New Testament...*Thou shalt not steal.*

Now we live in an age with security cameras, it is making it harder to steal from shops, and from one another. But we all have to be on our guard over identity theft which is becoming rife during this age of technology where there are little measures in place to stop this.

However this is the only one of two commandments that are made into civil law.
1. Thou shalt not kill.
2. Thou shalt not steal.

Both of these commandments are of punishable offence, and lead to a term in prison defined by the Judge and the court of civil law.

In Philippians 2:4...

Look not every man on his own things, but everyman also on the things of others.

In other words do not look at the things that other people possess, but to things that reflect the creation of God, and to come to worship God for he is our creator.

The more we look to God we realise that it is God that always provides for us, and so there is no need to steal. We just need to put our faith and trust in our creator, as he gives us everything that we need in order to survive in this life

9. Lying

The full power of God can be felt today as the wind and the rain beats down upon us. Oh what a marvellous sight it is, when one feels the full force of the wind as one crosses the road.

But sadly a majority of people moan, and refuse to accept it is our creator that is showing us he is still here and in control. The same was said after the ninth commandment was given to Moses...*Thou shalt not bear false witness against thy neighbour.* And again in Romans 13:9...*Thou shalt not bear false witness.*

People accept these commandments at first then continued to break it and denying it is from God.

However a few people do not fully understand what damage can be done by not obeying this commandment. It can cause a lot of grief and hurt. Lying can destroy; the words that come out of a lie can be painful.

In Psalms 12 David talks about the words that we speak and what damage they can do even when we lie.

David tells us...

Help, Lord; for the godly man ceaseth; for the faithful fail from among the children of men.
They speak vanity everyone with his neighbour: with flattering lips and with a double heart do they speak.
The Lord shall cut off all flattering lips, and the tongue that speaketh proud things:
Who have said, with our tongue will we prevail; our lips are our own: Who is Lord over us?
For the oppression of the poor, for the sighing of the needy, now will I arise, smith the Lord; I will set him in safety from him that puffed at him.
The words of the Lord are pure words: as silver tried in a furnace of earth purified seven times.
Thou salt keep them, O Lord, thou salt preserve them from this generation forever.
The wicked walk on every side, when the vilest men are exalted.

Lies are all part of what the Devil wants. He wants us to lie and speak lies. He also wants false teachers to lie and to hide the truth of eternal life. The gift that God has given to all of us who follow and obey him.

In Isaiah 45:18-22...

For thus saith the Lord that created the heavens; God himself that formed the earth and made it he hath established it, he created it not in vain, he formed it to be inhabited: I am the Lord; and there is none else.
I have not spoken in secret, in a dark place of the earth: I said not unto the seed of Jacob, Seek ye me in vain: I the Lord speak righteousness, I declare things that are right.
Assemble yourselves and come, draw near together, ye that are escaped of the nations: They have no knowledge that set up the wood of their graven image, and pray unto a God that cannot save.
Tell ye, and bring them near; yea, let them take counsel together: Who hath declared from this ancient time? Who hath told it from that time? Have not I the Lord? And there is no God else beside me; a just God and a Saviour; there is none beside me.
Look into me, and be ye saved, all the ends of the Earth: For I am God, and there is none else.

So we all have to stop listening to lies and rebuke them as God has just told us. We need to start reading and listening to the truth that is written in the Bible.

As one day all the lies and the words that are ever spoken will be judged. So beware you have been warned, start to tell the truth. Leave the lies to those who wish to go to Hell with the Devil and his demons because that is where liars are going to go.

As it is written in Revelation 21:8...

But the fearful, and unbelieving, and the abominable, and murderers, and whoremongers, and sorcerers and idolaters, and all liars, shall have their part in the lake which burneth with fire and brimstone.

10. Greed

Today it is want, want, want. We are all guilty of this. The Devil has ensured this by putting the desires of all things made by man into our faces, via television, radio, Internet, newspapers, technology and looking to what our neighbour has next door.

The final commandment given to Moses tells us it is a sin, a breaking of God's commandment if we are greedy.

As it is written...

Thou shalt not covet thy neighbour's house; thou shalt not covet thy neighbour's wife, nor his manservant, nor his maidservant, nor his ox, nor his ass, nor anything that is thy neighbours.

And again in Romans 7:7...*Thou shalt not covet.*

How many of us actually talk to our neighbour, get to know our neighbours and love our neighbours. Not many people would say that they know their neighbour, let alone love them. But because of greed we all strive to be better than our neighbour instead of loving our neighbour, and getting to know him or her.

It is written in Deuteronomy 10:17-19...

For the Lord your God is God of gods, and Lord of Lords, a great God, a mighty, and a terrible, which regardeth not persons, nor taketh reward:
He doth execute the judgement of the fatherless and widow, and loveth the stranger, in giving him food and raiment.
Love ye therefore the stranger: For ye were strangers in the land of Egypt. However our neighbours are our strangers and God tells us to love them as we love God.

Deuteronomy 11:1...

Therefore thou shalt love the Lord, thy God, and keep his charge, and his statutes, and his judgements, and his commandments always.

John 15:12...

This is my commandment, that ye love one another as I have loved you.

Thus, let us talk to our neighbours, get to know them and love them. For this is what is commanded. Only the Devil wants us to be greedy and covet the neighbour's house and all that he has.

The Ten Commandments are fundamental to our walk with the Lord Jesus and in obedience to God. When we break one of these commandments it is as if we have broken the whole of the laws of God and it is then that we must ask God for repentance and forgiveness as we put our sins to him.

Categories of Law

This chapter looks into detail the different categories of law as given to us from God in his word. Moral law is in the eternal and holy nature of God and as it relates to the nature of creation in its various moral estates, it is the foundation for all other categories we speak of in connection with law.

Therefore it is common to divide the law into three categories: moral, ceremonial and judicial in other words civil. The ceremonial laws were instituted to reveal the redemptive work of Christ in restoring fallen men to a right standing under the moral law, and the judicial, civil is exemplary of how moral law ought to govern human society.

1. Moral Law

The moral law shows us what is holy and condemns us when we are unholy. In this sense it readies us for God's work of redemption. God decreed that not all humans would continue in their fallen condition.

To display his grace, He ensured that a Messiah would come to take the place of his people in suffering their penalty and in meeting all the demands of divine holiness and justice for them. The details of God's work are revealed progressively from the expulsion from Eden all the way to the completion of the New Testament.

2. Ceremonial Law

Ceremonial law is where God prepares his people to understand what he would do to rescue them from sin, God imposed a whole set of regulations at Sinai. The temporal laws *"prefiguring the work of Jesus Christ as Redeemer"* are often called ceremonial laws.

When God led the children of Israel out of Egyptian bondage, He had given them the Ten Commandments. This Holy law was spoken by God, written by God, recorded on tables of stone, and is to last forever. At the same time the ceremonial law, was also delivered to the children of Israel.

This law dealt with the ceremonial rites of the Jews which then passed away at the cross. The books of Exodus, Leviticus, Numbers and Deuteronomy in the Old Testament describe in detail the ceremonial law.

Ceremonial law shows the importance of circumcision, sacrifices, offerings, purifications, holy days, and other rites that are written in the books of Exodus, Leviticus, Numbers and Deuteronomy.

God's Word speaks of two great Laws.

1. Law of God (the Ten Commandments) and also known by many as the Moral law.

2. Law of Moses (the Covenant"), this is also better known as the Mosaic Law, the Ordinances and the Ceremonial Law.

Is there a relationship between the Ten Commandments and the Ceremonial law?

There is a relationship between the Ten Commandments and the ceremonial law. When an Israelite sins; he is breaking the Ten Commandments, the Moral Law. He then has to bring his offering according to Law God Moses, the Sacrificial Law to receive forgiveness.

The relationship between these two laws are as follows, the Law of God defines sin, as sin is the transgression of the Moral Law, 1 John 3:4; *"Everyone doing sin also does lawlessness, and sin is lawlessness."*

The law of Moses is for the sacrifices, the Mosaic Law, the Ceremonial Law or Ordinances which are written as the original remedy for sin.

When the Israelite sinned, he had to make atonement for his sin. And in doing so he had to obey the second law.

We can clearly see here that there are two very distinct laws. It is the sacrifice that Jesus Christ had paid on the cross that permanently took the place of Law Number 2 when He cried out "*It is finished"* and bowed His head and died.

When the unseen hand of God had tore the temple curtain from top to bottom Matthew 27:51; "*And behold, the veil of the temple was split into two from above downwards, and the earth quaked, and the massive rocks split,"* this signified that this ceremonial law system was once and for all nailed to the cross when Jesus had died.

In the Bible we see that the word ceremonial is spoken frequently of and yet the term Ceremonial Law is not.

The ceremonial law was originally meant to be for Israel alone as the Gospel did not go to the Gentiles for 3.5 years after Jesus had died on the cross. The sacrifice that Jesus had paid ended this sacrificial system once and for all,.

We can be thankful that there is now no longer any requirement to obey this law of bondage which points forward to the true sacrifice carried out by our Redeemer that saves us from our Sins, which are transgressions of the Moral law, the Ten Commandments of love.

When we sin now, and we genuinely repent, it is through God's Grace and our faith in Jesus, that we are forgiven.

What is ceremonial law?

Ceremonial law can firstly be defined as the sequence of days observed for the feasts. This is shown very clearly in the Scriptures.

Leviticus 23:3 "*Six days shall work be done: but the seventh day is the Sabbath of rest, an holy convocation; you shall do no work therein: it is the SABBATH of the LORD in all your dwellings."*

The above verse refers to the fourth Commandment, i.e. Gods Sabbath. It is the "Sabbath of the Lord" and is part of the eternal law of love.

Sabbath is a day intended for fellowship with other Christians and meant for spending quality Holy time with our Creator. This is NOT part of the ceremonial law.

The seventh day Sabbath is a memorial of creation that God established at creation. Although it was celebrated as a feast day, it is not a day that originated with the Jews, it preceded them. When one of the feast days fell on the seventh day Sabbath, it was referred to as a high Sabbath day John 19:31; *"Therefore the Jews, since it was the preparation, that the bodies might not remain upon the cross in the Sabbath (because that Sabbath was a great day) requested Pilate that their legs be broken, and be taken away."*

Leviticus 23:4-5 "*These are the feasts of the LORD, even holy convocations, which you shall proclaim in their seasons.*
5 In the fourteenth day of the first month at even is the LORD'S Passover."

This part of the ceremonial law was a shadow of Jesus crucifixion and is called "Passover or Pesach."

Leviticus 23:6-8 *"And on the fifteenth day of the same month is the feast of unleavened bread unto the LORD: seven days you must eat unleavened bread.*
7 In the first day you shall have an holy convocation: you shall do no servile work therein.
8 But you shall offer an offering made by fire unto the LORD seven days: in the seventh day is an holy convocation: you shall do no servile work therein."

This part of the ceremonial law shows the time Jesus spent in the tomb on the seventh day Sabbath and is called the "Feast of Unleavened Bread."

The Feast of Unleavened Bread shows the sinless nature of Jesus, releasing us from the bondage of sin. Jesus is the sinless bread of life.

John 6:32, *"Therefore Jesus said to them, Amen, amen, I say to you, Moses absolutely did not give you the bread out of heaven, but my Father gives you the true bread out of heaven,"*

John 6: 48-51; *"I am the bread of life.*
49 Your fathers ate manna in the wasteland, and died.
50 This is the bread coming down out of heaven that anyone may eat of it and not die.
51 I am the living bread which came down out of heaven; if anyone eats of this bread, he will live forever, and also the bread which I will give is my flesh, which I will give for the life of the world."

And leavened bread represented the corruption of sin in one's life that Jesus overcame for us.

1 Corinthians 5:8; *"Therefore let us observe the feast, not in old leaven, neither in the leaven of malice and depravity, but in the unleavened bread of purity and truth."*

Putting away the sin in our lives (leavened bread) and replacing it by accepting sinless Jesus Christ (unleavened bread) in its place is the Gospel Message. This is now known as the Passover meal, the Lord's Supper or Communion.

When we participate in the Lord's Supper we do this to remember the sacrifice that Jesus made for us at the cross.

Luke 22:19; *"And taking bread, having given thanks, he broke it, and gave to them, saying, This is my body which is given for you; do this in remembrance of me."*

This was the time of year of the latter rain (March/April). On this day as recorded in the Bible Israel began to eat from the old corn and the manna which ended the following day.

Joshua 5:11; *"And they ate of the stored grain of the land on the next day of the Passover, unleavened and toasted cakes in this same day."*

Leviticus 23:9-14 *"And the LORD spoke unto Moses, saying,*
10 Speak unto the children of Israel, and say unto them, When you be come into the land which I give unto you, and shall reap the harvest thereof, then you shall bring a sheaf of the first fruits of your harvest unto the priest:
11 And he shall wave the sheaf before the LORD, to be accepted for you: on the morrow after the Sabbath the priest shall wave it.
12 And you shall offer that day when you wave the sheaf an he lamb without blemish of the first year for a burnt offering unto the LORD.
13 And the meat offering thereof shall be two tenth deals of fine flour mingled with oil, an offering made by fire unto the LORD for a sweet savour: and the drink offering thereof shall be of wine, the fourth part of an hin.
14 And you shall eat neither bread, nor parched corn, nor green ears, until the selfsame day that you have brought an offering unto your God: it shall be a statute for ever throughout your generations in all your dwellings."

This part of the ceremonial law represents Jesus' resurrection from the tomb and is called "First Fruits."

This was the day of first sheaf waving, the first fruit of the barley harvest.

Jesus was the first fruits of the resurrection,

1 Corinthians 15:20, *"And now Christ has been raised out of the dead, and became the first fruits of those fallen asleep,"*

1 Corinthians 15: 23, *"And everyone in his own order: Christ the first fruits, afterward they who are Christ's in his coming to be at our side,"*

2 Timothy 2:6-8, *"The farmer toiling must be the first to partake of the fruits.*
7 Exercise your mind on what I say, because the Lord will give you understanding in all things.
8 Remember, Jesus Christ out of the seed of David was raised out of the dead according to my good news,"

This is the festival of Sabbaths. They are not just commemorative in nature but also prophetic, pointing to future Holy events as fulfilments.

To suggest a new Sunday holy day was instituted on resurrection day, is to say the festival calendar appointed by God was in error since it omits a weekly 1st day observance.

In Jewish Tradition, the period called the Omer begins on 16 Nisan and extends for 50 days to Pentecost or Shavuot. Manna ceased to fall on this day.

Joshua 5:12; *"And the manna ceased on the next day after they had eaten of the stored grain of the land, and there was not any more manna to the children of Israel, and they ate of the produce of the land of Canaan that year."*

Leviticus 23:15-21 *"And you shall count unto you from the morrow after the Sabbath, from the day that you brought the sheaf of the wave offering; seven Sabbaths shall be complete:*
16 Even unto the morrow after the seventh Sabbath shall you number fifty days; and you shall offer a new meat offering unto the LORD.

17 You shall bring out of your habitations two wave loaves of two tenth deals: they shall be of fine flour; they shall be baken with leaven; they are the first fruits unto the LORD.
18 And you shall offer with the bread seven lambs without blemish of the first year, and one young bullock, and two rams: they shall be for a burnt offering unto the LORD, with their meat offering, and their drink offerings, even an offering made by fire, of sweet savour unto the LORD.
19 Then you shall sacrifice one kid of the goats for a sin offering, and two lambs of the first year for a sacrifice of peace offerings.
20 And the priest shall wave them with the bread of the first fruits for a wave offering before the LORD, with the two lambs: they shall be holy to the LORD for the priest.
21 And you shall proclaim on the selfsame day, that it may be an holy convocation unto you: you shall do no servile work therein: it shall be a statute for ever in all your dwellings throughout your generations."

This represents Pentecost and is called the "Feast of Weeks or Shavuot."

This feast also represents the fifty days after the resurrection, when there was the first outpouring of the Holy Spirit that resulted in three thousand souls being added to the church in one day

Acts 2:41; *"Therefore those gladly receiving his word were baptized, and that day there were added about three thousand souls."*

This outpouring of the Holy Spirit is also known as the early rain. There will also be a latter rain, the greater outpouring of the Holy Spirit nearer to the end time

Joel 2:23, *"And you children of Zion, spin around in emotion, and rejoice in Jehovah your God, because he has given you the rain for planting just right, and he will cause the rain to descend for you, the rain for planting, and the rain for harvest in the first new moon."*

Zechariah 10:1, *"Ask of Jehovah rain in the time of the harvest rain; Jehovah shall make lightning's, and give them showers of rain, to give to every man the plant in the field,"*

James 5:7; *"Therefore be patient, brothers, until the coming of the Lord to be at our side. Behold, the farmer waits for the highly valued fruit of the earth, and has patience upon it until he takes the autumn rain and the later rain."*

Leviticus 23:23-25 *"And the LORD spoke unto Moses, saying,*
24 Speak unto the children of Israel, saying, In the seventh month, in the first day of the month, shall you have a Sabbath, a memorial of blowing of trumpets, an holy convocation.
25 You shall do no servile work therein: but you shall offer an offering made by fire unto the LORD."

This passage of Scripture refers to the Day of Judgment and is also the Jewish New Year. It is called "Trumpets or Rosh Ha-Shanna."

This announcement to Israel informed the Israelites of any impending judgment which occurred on the Day of Atonement nine days later. The Trumpets acted as a worldwide proclamation of the second coming in 1843, during the "Great Awakening" revival which is based on the 2300 days prophecy in Daniel 8:14; *"And he said to me, Unto dusk to dawn, two thousand and three hundred, and the sanctuary shall be vindicated as right."*

This started in 457 B.C. and ended in 1844. Many people alive during the year 1844 mistakenly interpreted this as the time of the second coming and end of the world, when in fact it was the cleansing of the heavenly sanctuary.

Leviticus 23:26-32 *"And the LORD spoke unto Moses, saying,*
27 Also on the tenth day of this seventh month there shall be a day of atonement: it shall be an holy convocation unto you; and you shall afflict your souls, and offer an offering made by fire unto the LORD.
28 And you shall do no work in that same day: for it is a day of atonement, to make an atonement for you before the LORD your God.
29 For whatsoever soul it be that shall not be afflicted in that same day, he shall be cut off from among his people.
30 And whatsoever soul it be that doeth any work in that same day, the same soul will I destroy from among his people.
31 You shall do no manner of work: it shall be a statute for ever throughout your generations in all your dwellings.
32 It shall be unto you a Sabbath of rest, and you shall afflict your souls: in the ninth day of the month at even, from even unto even, shall you celebrate your Sabbath."

This passage represents a very important part of the ceremonial law and is called the "Day of Atonement or Yom Kippur."

This is the Holiest day of the year and signifies a cleansing of sins and reconciliation with God (Judgment day). The people were to afflict their souls and fast. On this day only the High Priest enter the Holy place to atone the sins of the people.

We can also see Jesus carrying out His role as our High Priest and entering the Holy of Holies in the heavenly sanctuary when he began the investigative judgment at the end of the 2300 days of Daniel 8:14; *"And he said to me, Unto dusk to dawn, two thousand and three hundred, and the sanctuary shall be vindicated as right."*

This is the beginning of the fulfilment of the Day of Atonement which is still underway in heaven today. Many do not understand this judgment and so they condemn it.

What they fail to realize in so doing is that they take away the purpose and fulfilment of this day and hence remove the notion of the whole Old Testament's purpose of this Holy day and it pointing forward to Jesus who is now our High Priest and fulfilment here.

This judgment begins with the righteous who are already dead and will end with the righteous living. At the end of this period of judgment, probation for humanity will have closed, and the 7 plagues of God will then fall upon the wicked.

After this will be the second coming to gather the righteous, so that they too can join the kingdom of God in heaven for 1000 years.

The Jubilee year begins on this day.

Leviticus 25:9; *"And you shall cause the trumpet of shouting of joy to crossover on the tenth of the seventh new moon, the day of covering; you shall make the trumpet to cross over your whole land."*

Leviticus 23:33-44 *"And the LORD spoke unto Moses, saying,*
34 Speak unto the children of Israel, saying, The fifteenth day of this seventh month shall be the feast of tabernacles for seven days unto the LORD.
35 On the first day shall be an holy convocation: you shall do no servile work therein.

36 Seven days you shall offer an offering made by fire unto the LORD: on the eighth day shall be an holy convocation unto you; and you shall offer an offering made by fire unto the LORD: it is a solemn assembly; and you shall do no servile work therein.
37 These are the feasts of the LORD, which you shall proclaim to be holy convocations, to offer an offering made by fire unto the LORD, a burnt offering, and a meat offering, a sacrifice, and drink offerings, every thing upon his day:
38 Beside the Sabbaths of the LORD, and beside your gifts, and beside all your vows, and beside all your freewill offerings, which you give unto the LORD.
39 Also in the fifteenth day of the seventh month, when you have gathered in the fruit of the land, you shall keep a feast unto the LORD seven days: on the first day shall be a Sabbath, and on the eighth day shall be a Sabbath.
40 And you shall take you on the first day the boughs of goodly trees, branches of palm trees, and the boughs of thick trees, and willows of the brook; and you shall rejoice before the LORD your God seven days.
41 And you shall keep it a feast unto the LORD seven days in the year. It shall be a statute for ever in your generations: you shall celebrate it in the seventh month.
42 You shall dwell in booths seven days; all that are Israelites born shall dwell in booths:
43 That your generations may know that I made the children of Israel to dwell in booths, when I brought them out of the land of Egypt: I am the LORD your God.
44 And Moses declared unto the children of Israel the feasts of the LORD."

This final feast is called the "Feast of Tabernacles or Sukkoth."

For seven days the people moved out of their homes and lived in temporary shelters called "Sukkah" as a reminder of their wanderings in the desert for forty years. The branches cut from palm, willow and other trees were to be waved in celebration to the Lord during the first seven days of the feast.

Leviticus 23:40; *"And you shall take to yourself on the first day the fruit of magnificent trees, palms of palm trees, and the boughs of thick trees, and willows of the stream, and you shall rejoice before the face of Jehovah your God seven days."*

This final feast of the year is a celebration of ingathering at the end of the harvest Exodus 23:16; *"And the feast of harvest, the first fruits of your labours, which you have sown in the field, and the feast of ingathering, in the going out of the year, when you have gathered in your labours out of the field."* and is a time of rejoicing and fellowship.

It symbolizes the gathering or harvest of God's people who leave earth for the marriage supper of the Lamb to be celebrated in heaven after the second coming of Jesus.

Then the millennium begins.

However, some of those temporal laws were originally intended to set apart the people of Israel from the rest of humanity. These laws included dietary regulations, purification methods, ordinances about the design of their clothes, and other daily matters that marked them out from the Gentiles.

The distinguishing of Israel showed how God by His grace called some to salvation. It was not the same as the election of some to eternal life and regeneration. It exemplified it. Other temporal laws were imposed to regulate a system of sacrifices and temple worship.

These were designed to demonstrate the special work of the Messiah as the Lamb of God who had came to suffer, to live a perfectly holy life, and to give his life as a payment for sin on behalf of those God had decreed to save.

We can clearly see that the purpose of these temporal laws was to show the work of redemption and the consequences of violating moral law. It also shows how God would restore some who had fallen into sin.

When the work was accomplished in history, these regulations no longer had a purpose and a meaning. As a consequence they were set aside by direct revelation from the God who imposed them.

Judicial Law

Judicial Law is written as follows:

1. God, the Supreme Lord and King of the entire world, hath ordained civil magistrates to be under him over the people, for his own glory and the public good; and to this end, hath armed them with the power of the sword, for the defence and encouragement of them that are good, and for the punishment of evildoers.

2. It is lawful for Christians to accept and execute the office of a magistrate when called thereunto; in the managing whereof, as they ought especially to maintain piety, justice, and peace, according to the wholesome laws of each commonwealth, so, for that end, they may lawfully, now under the New Testament, wage war upon just and necessary occasions.

3. Civil magistrates may not assume to themselves the administration of the Word and Sacraments; or the power of the keys of the kingdom of heaven; or, in the least, interfere in matters Westminster Confession of Faith Anonymous of faith.

Yet, as nursing fathers, it is the duty of civil magistrates to protect the church of our common Lord, without giving the preference to any denomination of Christians above the rest, in such a manner that all ecclesiastical persons whatever shall enjoy the full, free, and unquestioned liberty of discharging every part of their sacred functions, without violence or danger.

And, as Jesus Christ hath appointed a regular government and discipline in his church, no law of any commonwealth should interfere with, let, or hinder, the due exercise thereof, among the voluntary members of any denomination of Christians, according to their own profession of belief.

It is the duty of civil magistrates to protect the person and good name of all their people, in such an effectual manner as that no person be suffered, either upon pretence of religion or infidelity, to offer any indignity, violence, abuse, or injury to any other person whatsoever: and to take order, that all religious and ecclesiastical assemblies be held without molestation or disturbance.

4. It is the duty of the people to pray for magistrates, to honour their persons, to pay them tribute and other dues, to obey their lawful commands, and to be subject to their authority, for conscience' sake.

Infidelity, or difference in religion, doth not make bode the magistrate's just and legal authority, nor free the people from their obedience to him: from which ecclesiastical persons are not exempted; much less hath the Pope any power or jurisdiction over them in their dominions, or over any of their people; and least of all to deprive them of their dominions or lives, if he shall judge them to be heretics, or upon any other pretence whatsoever.

We can see that the Westminster Confession describes a category of law which God gave to ancient Israel as a body politic. They were for the ordering of a godly society.

These regulations were called judicial because they directed the civil magistrates in determining whether a person was of guilt or of innocence in those who were accused of crimes, and in imposing just penalties upon those found guilty.

These regulations are not in themselves moral law. These regulations showed what moral law looked like when applied to specific cases of abuse. They are not ceremonial because they were not illustrative of the work of redemption except in showing the need for satisfying the eternal principle of justice.

The Westminster Confession states that various judicial laws expired along with the special place of Israel as God's covenant nation. They were given at Sinai showing the Levitical order of the rule of Elders and Priests who served on both spiritual and civil courts as shepherds of God's people.

Many of the procedures described in them relates to the authority structure of the sacrificial system and of the specific tribes who were assigned duties within the covenant nation. Then when this was completed the work of atonement and the rejection of Israel as God's special covenant people, many of the details of these laws, which were connected with the ceremonial system seem to have became obsolete.

The Westminster Confession adds that, though some details of certain judicial laws expired, there remains an obligation required by general equity. General equity is a legal term taken from English law.

There is however obvious difficulties that arise in identifying the principles of general equity that are expressed in particular judicial laws and in properly knowing how to put them into practice today.

The specific form that the judicial laws took were mainly by the technological advances of the day and by the methods of construction, means of transportation, standards of measurement, tools for agriculture, and other matters as according to the age in which the laws were written.

It is our duty to identify and maintain the general principles expressed in judicial law while recognizing the changes that had taken place. Therefore it is important that we need to consider the following:

1. The ending of the civil structure of ancient Israel. When God had finally judged her as a nation, and removed her place as His covenant people

2. The completion of; and the atonement by Jesus Christ who eliminated the need of a sacrificial system and the authority structure associated with it

3. The changes made in technology and customs regarding the regulation of particular practices.

Therefore it is important to not that we must remain in obedience to God and his word, and that when we fail we are to return to repentance and ask God to forgive us of that sin.

God's law in today's society

This chapter looks at God's law in today's society and how it applies to every one of us.

How Does God's Law Apply Today?

There are statements in the New Testament that explain how certain aspects of God's law are now fulfilled with the completion of the work of Jesus Christ and the removal of Israel as God's special covenant people.

Matthew 5:17-20; *"Do not suppose that I came to loosen down the law or the prophets; I absolutely did not come to loosen down, but to fulfil.*
18 Because, Amen, I say to you, until heaven and earth pass away, one iota or one particle will absolutely not pass away from the law until all comes to be.
19 Whoever therefore will make one of these least commandments loose, and teaches men in this way, he shall be called the least in the kingdom of heaven, and whoever does and teaches them, this one will be called great in the kingdom of heaven.
20 Because I say to you that, unless your righteousness shall excel in superiority that of the scribes and Pharisees, you shall absolutely not enter into the kingdom of heaven."

In this scripture we can see that the ancient sects of the Scribes and Pharisees had departed from the law of God and confused its use. They made it into a superficial set of regulations which they saw as a means of salvation, and as a cause for personal pride and fundamentalism.

Jesus explained to them how their attitude towards the law was wrong. The context of this passage contrasts their perversions of moral law with what God had actually said and intended.

He said...

Matthew 5:17-20; *"Do not suppose that I came to loosen down the law or the prophets; I absolutely did not come to loosen down, but to fulfil.*
18 Because, Amen, I say to you, until heaven and earth pass away, one iota or one particle will absolutely not pass away from the law until all comes to be.
19 Whoever therefore will make one of these least commandments loose, and teaches men in this way, he shall be called the least in the kingdom of heaven, and whoever does and teaches them, this one will be called great in the kingdom of heaven.
20 Because I say to you that, unless your righteousness shall excel in superiority that of the scribes and Pharisees, you shall absolutely not enter into the kingdom of heaven."

Jesus denied that his coming was intended to abolish or to destroy the law or the words of the prophets. The term he uses in 5:17 is (katalu-o) in Greek which means to throw down, destroy, demolish, abolish or annul.

He immediately added the positive side, to what his purpose regarding the law was. He came to fulfil it. The word he used for fulfil is (plaerosai), in Greek which means to fulfil, accomplish, complete or to bring something to its full measure.

Jesus accomplished this threefold:

1. As a Prophet he brought the law to it fullest revelation by showing us the meaning underlying the

symbols and practices of the ceremonial law.

2. As a Priest he was the Sacrificial Lamb satisfying the demands of the law in the place of his people. He represented them both in the keeping of the law perfectly, and in the suffering and dying to satisfy the demands of divine justice for their sin.

3. As a King he pronounced the curse of the law upon those who remain the enemies of God and of God's kingdom.

The perplexity of the law is compared with the persistence of the created universe. Beginning with the solemn declaration "truly" (amhn) in Greek, he said that the law would last as long as the universe lasts.

It would remain until the heaven and earth pass away. Those who imagine that Jesus was declaring the elimination of the law have but to observe the stars and mountains to know that it has not yet taken place.

He then showed that the law as a whole persists. Not even the smallest parts were being cancelled out. He has shown us with references to the different forms of letters in the Hebrew alphabet, the language of the law and the Old Testament.

Yet the Gospel writer illustrates it in Greek.

Jesus is appeared as the least in the Kingdom of Heaven.

The rabbis had divided the law into 613 commandments. They identified 248 of them as stated positively and 365 as stated negatively. They debated on what were the heavier or lighter of the commandments.

According to many the lightest was found in Deuteronomy 22:6-7 which says *that if you find a bird's nest with young or eggs, and the mother of the bird is with them, you may take the eggs but you may not take the mother.*

The weightiest was generally shown to be found in Deuteronomy 6:5 which requires that *we love the Lord our God with all our heart, soul and might.*

In Luke 10:27-28; *"And he answering said, You shall love the Lord your God out of all your heart, and out of all your soul, and out of all your strength, and out of all the exercise of your mind, and your neighbour as yourself. And he said to him, you have answered correctly; do this, and you will live."*

We can see in this passage that Jesus accepted this answer when it was offered to him by an expert in the law.

Jesus' comments clarify what he meant by not coming to destroy the law but to fulfil it. All the points of God's moral law, expanded upon in Matthew 5:21-48, *"You heard that it has been spoken to the ancients, absolutely do not murder, and whoever murders shall be liable in the judgment;*
22 And I say to you, That everyone who is provoked to anger with his brother without cause shall be liable in the judgment, and whoever says to his brother, You are bad, shall be liable to the Sanhedrin, and whoever says, Fool, shall be liable to hell fire.
23 If therefore you offer your gift upon the altar, and there remember that your brother has anything against you,

24 Leave there your gift in front of the altar, and go away; first be reconciled to your brother, and then coming, offer your gift.
25 In haste be in a good mind with your opponent while you are with him in the way, lest at any time the opponent gives you over to the judge, and the judge to the subordinate officer, and you be thrown into prison.
26 Amen, I say to you, You will absolutely not at all come out of there until you pay the last kodrantes.
27 You heard that it was spoken to the ancients; absolutely do not commit adultery;
28 And I say to you, that everyone looking at a woman to set his passion upon her has committed adultery with her already in his heart.
29 And if your right eye offends you, tear it out, and throw it from you, because it is advantageous for you that one of your members should be destroyed, and not your whole body be thrown into hell.
30 And if your right hand offends you, chop it off, and throw it from you, because it is advantageous for you that one of your members should be destroyed, and not your whole body be thrown into hell.
31 And it was spoken; whoever sets free his wife, let him give her a divorce;
32 And I say to you, that whoever sets free his wife without the word of sexual promiscuity makes her commit adultery, and whoever shall marry the one set free commits adultery.
33 Again, you have heard that it has been spoken to the ancients, absolutely do not commit perjury, but give over your oaths to the Lord;
34 And I say to you, do not swear at all, not even by the heaven, because it is his throne;
35 Not even by the earth, because it is the footstool of his feet; not even by Jerusalem, because it is the city of the great King.
36 Do not even swear by your head, because you absolutely do not have power to make one hair white or black.
37 And let your word be, Yes, yes; no, no, and whatever is more than these is out of the evil one.
38 You heard that it was spoken, An eye for an eye, and a tooth for a tooth;
39 And I say to you, Do not stand against the evil, but whoever slaps you on your right cheek, turn around to him also the other.
40 And the one deciding to sue you and take away your tunic, let him also take your cloak.
41 And whoever will compel you into public service one mile, go on with him two.
42 Give to the one asking you, and from the one deciding to borrow from you, do not turn away.
43 You heard that it was spoken, You shall love your neighbour, and shall hate the one who hates you.
44 And I say to you, Love those hating you; bless those cursing you; do good to those hating you, and pray over those abusing you and pursuing you,
45 So that you may be children of your Father in heaven, because he causes his sun to rise on the evil and on the inherently good, and showers on the righteous and on the unrighteous.
46 Because if you love those loving you, what reward do you have? Do absolutely not even the tax collectors do the same?
47 And if you embrace your brothers only, what more than is required are you doing? Do the tax collectors absolutely not do the same?
48 You therefore be perfect even as your Father in heaven is perfect."

We can see here that they are ongoing and are not annulled or set aside in the coming of Jesus as the Messiah. Jesus came to complete the law for us, not to take it away.

We must lay hold of the law in its true sense, as a moral and continual revelation of God's commanded holiness. This ought to make us live more honourably to the Lord who has transformed us by grace, than those hypocritical critics, the Scribes and Pharisees.

Though Jesus seemed to disobey the law, it was really only the perverted interpretations of the law which the corrupted rabbis had proposed that he disobeyed. He did not abolish the law by fulfilling it. This is directly denied by his own words. Instead of abolishing the law he fulfilled it.

Romans 10:4; *"For Christ is the end of the law for righteousness to everyone who believes."*

While Jesus used the word (plaerosai) in Greek meaning that he came to fulfil the law, Paul uses another word. He says that Jesus, in his accomplishing his work or redemption, has become the (telos) in Greek of the law. He is the end of the law.

We see that from this concept of fulfilling its true meaning, which means to bring something to its full measure. Being the end of the law means to bring it to its goal, to its intended end product.

This same word (telos) in Greek is used by Peter in salvation faith.

1 Peter 1:9 *"Obtaining as the OUTCOME (telos) of your faith the salvation of your souls."*

Certainly Peter did not mean that the salvation of our souls comes by eliminating our faith. The meaning of the word end would be completely out of place. Salvation is what faith comes about as its fruit in us. It is the goal of our belief in the promise of the gospel.

Jesus is no more eliminating the law, which our salvation comes by the eliminating of our faith. This is simply not the meaning of the word used here. Jesus may by many be said to be the outcome of the law. He is what the law was directing us to do and ensuring that we love and obey it. He is the goal of the law.

The law shows our sin and failure to have righteousness on our own. It shows us how Jesus lived a holy life in our place. It convicts the regenerated soul and drives it to the Saviour. Jesus used this same word on the cross.

John records how Jesus completed the work the Father had given him. He had reached the goal of the promise of the covenant of redemption.

John 19:30 When Jesus therefore had received the sour wine, He said, *"It is finished!"*

The word used by Jesus for finished is (tetelestai) in Greek, from this same word (telos). Jesus was indicating not that it's over. But that the work he came to do was finished, completed, and consummated.

The writer of Hebrews uses the same work of the completion of our salvation in Christ in Hebrews 6:1; *"Therefore leaving the beginning of the word about the Christ, let us be carried on to the Perfecta, not again laying down the foundation of repentance from dead works, and of faith upon God,"* and Hebrews 10:14; *"Because by one offering he has perfected forever those being sanctified."*

Jesus is the perfection of the law. He is its goal and end product. As our Saviour he accomplished what the law promised and made it possible that redeemed sinners would be enabled to live obediently with the glory of God as their true motivation.

Romans 10:4; *"For Christ is the end of the law for righteousness to everyone who believes."*

We can see from this passage of scripture that Jesus is not the cancellation of the law; he is not its cessation. He is "its completion, its goal, its consummate enablement, its perfecta." By his completed work he brings righteousness to all who believe.

The law is exalted by Paul. It is in no way degraded.

What is the importance of the Law of God for believers living in this age?

Here is a summary of the importance of the Law of God living in this age and in a society that is so far from God that no one thinks twice about breaking his laws and commandments.

1. God's moral law reveals what is pleasing to the Eternal King.

It shows us what is right and true. The revealing of the nature of God is presented in the Bible as a prime purpose of all things He had made.

Psalm 19:1-6; *"The heavens tally up the heavy glory of God, and the firmament causes the work of his hands to stand out boldly.*
2 Day to day gushes forth what he says, and night to night causes knowledge to live.
3 There is no speech, and there are no words where their voice is not heard.
4 Their measuring line is gone out through all the earth, and their discourse to the end of the inhabited earth. He has put a tent for the sun in them;
5 He is as a bridegroom coming out of his canopy, and will rejoice as a mighty man to run a path.
6 From the extremity of the heavens is his going forth, and his revolution to the ends of it, and there is nothing hid from his heat."

Romans 1:20; *"On this very account the invisible things of him from the creation of the world are clearly seen, being understood by the workmanship, both his eternal power and deity, into their being without excuse;"*

Therefore making himself known must also be a prime purpose of his specially revealed moral law. The more we understand God's law, the more we will respond with proper worship regarding his glory.

Psalm 119:27; *"The way of your visited mandates causes me to understand, and I shall ponder your wonders."*

2. God's law exposes our fallen nature and inability to please God.

The more we understand God's law, the more we are humbled before the perfectly pure holiness and justice of our Heavenly Father. It shows how unworthy we are of his blessing, and how impossible it is for us to keep the law sufficiently to please God, even in one little point.

Romans 7:7 *"What shall we say then? Is the Law sin? May it never be! On the contrary, I would not have come to know sin except through the Law; for I would not have known about coveting if the Law had not said, "You shall not covet."*

Romans 7:12 *"So then, the Law is holy, and the commandment is holy and righteous and good."*

3. God's law foreshadows the work of Jesus as the Messiah.

The ceremonial law dramatically shows us that our sin deserves death. It teaches us that unless God provides a substitute for his people by a gracious covenant, there is no hope for any of us. The symbolic animal sacrifices of the Old Testament foreshadowed the sacrifice of Jesus Christ.

Since the death of Jesus had been completed, the rituals of the Levitical code have ceased to have any real purpose. But what was required by divine justice remains, and this has not changed. Death for sin is required of everyone descending from Adam.

The only solution to conquer sin is found in the Bible where Jesus a perfect redeemer who is also the infinite God takes the position of being our living human sacrifice. The ritual laws continue to drive us to Christ as we study the principles underlying them which are made clear in the New Testament.

Galatians 3:24 *"Therefore the Law has become our tutor to lead us to Christ, that we may be justified by faith."*

2 Corinthians 5:21 *"he became sin for us ... that we be made the righteousness of God in him."*

Hebrews 9:12 *"and not through the blood of goats and calves, but through His own blood, He entered the holy place once for all, having obtained eternal redemption."*

Hebrews 10:4 *"For it is impossible for the blood of bulls and goats to take away sins."*

4. God's law is a perfect guide for showing us how we ought to live.

As believers we are made alive spiritually, compelling him by the renewed disposition of the heart, to give thankful obedience to our Saviour. The law of God shows what is pleasing to the object of our love. Otherwise we would not know how to honourably show our gratitude.

Psalm 119:9 *"How can a young man keep his way pure? By keeping it according to Thy word."*

Psalm 119:97 *"O how I love Thy law! It is my meditation all the day."*

Psalm 119:171 *"Let my lips utter praise, For Thou dost teach me Thy statutes."*

5. God's law restrains sin for the benefit of the covenant people.

The general effects of the law are applied by God to society in a general attempt to provide a restraining effect, which in other words keeps depravity from expanding into total moral chaos. Even ungodly societies have had some laws against murder, civil violence, theft, and such crimes would disrupt tranquillity in society.

Despite throughout history that it has been recorded that pagan societies may impose such laws thinking they only benefit themselves. We know that it is the merciful work of God who is the author of every good, and who brings forth even the unwitting service of his enemies.

Proverbs 19:21 *"Many are the plans in a man's heart, But the counsel of the Lord, it will stand."*

Proverbs 21:1 *"The king's heart is like channels of water in the hand of the LORD; He turns it wherever He wishes."*

God's law continues to have great uses and benefits today. Though some legal duties may have only temporal applications, there is an eternal element to all of God's law.

The moral principles underlying the revealed precepts are never done and will never go away. We need to learn to honour that law and to be holy even as the Lord our God is holy.

Therefore to conclude we need to consider ourselves to be dead to sin, separated from its mastery, and made alive to God who is the master of all righteousness.

We need to remove every opportunity for sinning and press on to improve holiness. We need to expect the promise of our Saviour to bring progressive victory using our prayers and honouring our grateful obedience.

God's law in men's hearts

Hebrews 8:10; *"For this is the covenant that I will make with the house of Israel after those days, saith the Lord; I will put my laws into their mind, and write them in their hearts."*

When God gave to Israel his law, the law of the first covenant, it was such a holy law that it ought to have been kept by the people. It was a just and righteous law, which God said, *"Ye shall do my judgments, and keep mine ordinances, to walk therein: I am the Lord your God. Ye shall therefore keep my statutes, and my judgments: which if a man do, he shall live in them: I am the Lord."*

The law of the Ten Commandments is strictly just; it is such a law as a man might make for himself if he studied his own best interests, and had wisdom enough to frame it aright.

It is a perfect law, in which the interests of God and man are both studied; it is not a partial law, but impartial, complete, and covering all the circumstances of life.

We could not take away one command out of the ten without spoiling both tables of the law, and we could not add another command without being guilty of making it superficial. The law is holy, and just, and good; it is like the God who made it, it is a perfect law. Then, surely, it ought to have been kept.

When men revolt against unjust laws, they are to be commended; but when a law is admitted to be perfect, then disobedience to it is an act of exceeding guilt.

Furthermore, God not only gave a law which ought to have been kept, because of its own intrinsic excellence, but he also gave it in a very wonderful way, which ought to have ensured its observance by the people.

The Lord came down upon Mount Sinai in fire, and the mountain was altogether on a smoke, and the smoke thereof ascended *"as the smoke of a furnace, and the whole mount Quaked greatly;"* and the sight that was then seen on Sinai, and the sounds that were there heard, and all the pomp and awful grandeur were so terrible that even Moses,—that boldest, calmest, quietest of men said, *"I do exceedingly fear and quake."*

The children of Israel, as they heard that law proclaimed, were so amazed and overwhelmed with God's display of his majesty and might, that they were ready enough to promise to keep his commandments.

The law of God could not have been made known to mankind in a grander or more sublime style than was displayed in the giving of that covenant on Mount Sinai.

After the giving of the law, did not God affix to it those terrible penalties which should have prevented men from disobeying his commands?

"Cursed is every one that continueth not in all things which are written in the book of the law to do them" "The soul that sinneth, it shall die."

It was the capital sentence that was to be pronounced upon the disobedient; there could be no heavier punishment than that. God had, as it were, drawn his sword against sin; and if man had been a reasonable being, he ought at once to have started back from committing an act which he might be sure would make God his foe.

Moreover, the blessings that were appended to the keeping of the law ought to have induced men to keep it; look again at those:

"Ye shall therefore keep my statutes, and my judgments: which if a man do, he shall live in them: I am the Lord."

This did not mean that the man who kept God's law should merely exist; there are some in these degenerate days who seek to make out life to be existence, and death to be annihilation, but there is little likeness between the words, or between what those words mean.

"He shall live in them," said the Lord concerning the man who kept his law; and there is a fullness of blessedness couched in that word, *"live."*

If men had kept the covenant of the Lord, if Adam, for instance, had kept it in the garden of Eden, the rose would have been without a thorn to tear his flesh, and the enjoyment of life would never have been marred by the bitterness of toil or grief.

But unfortunately as we have seen and been told in the bible all of these solemn sanctions of the ancient covenant, men did not keep it.

The promise, *"This do, and thou shalt live,"* never produced any doing that was worthy to be rewarded with life; and the threatening, *"Do this, and thou shalt die,"* never kept any man back from daringly venturing into the wrong road which leadeth unto death.

The fact is that the covenant of works, if it is looked upon as a way of safety, we can see that it is a total failure. No man ever persevered in it unto the end, and no man ever attained unto life by keeping it.

Nor can we, now that we are fallen, ever hope to be better than our un-fallen covenant-head, Adam; nor may we, who are already lost and condemned by our sinful works, dream for a moment that we shall be able to save ourselves by our works.

Therefore when we see, the first covenant was in these terms, *"You do right, and God will reward you for it. If you deserve life, God will give it to you."*

Now, as we all know right well, that covenant was broken all to pieces; it was unable to stand by reason of the weakness of our flesh and the corruptness of our nature. So God set aside that first covenant, he put it away as an outworn and useless thing; and he brought in a new covenant, the covenant of grace; and in our text we see what is the tenor of it: *"I will put my laws into their mind, and write them in their hearts."*

This is one of the most glorious promises that ever fell from the lips of infinite love. God didn't say, *"I will come again, as I came on Sinai, and thunder at them."* No, but, *"I will come in gentleness and mercy, and find a way into their hearts."*

God didn't say, *"I will take two great tables of stone, and with my finger write out my law before their eyes."* No, but, *"I will put my finger upon their hearts, and there will I write my law."*

God didn't say, *"I will give promises and threatenings that shall be the safeguard of this new covenant;"* but, *"I will with my Spirit graciously operate upon their minds and their hearts, and so I will sweetly influence them to serve me,—not for reward, nor from any servile motive, but because they know me, and they love me, and they feel it to be their delight to walk in the way of my commandments."*

Thus we must all be shares in the blessings of that new covenant!

In other words when God says this to us, and do this; and if we do what God asks, we shall meet him in the glory-land, to sing unto the grace of that eternal God who has wrought so wondrously with us, and in us, and for us!

What is the meaning of this blessing; "I will put my laws into their mind, and write them in their hearts."?

It means that when God comes to deal with his own chosen people, really to save them, he makes them know his law. The law still stands in the Old Testament, and our blessed Master, the Lord Jesus Christ, has condensed it into one word "Love;" and then he has expanded it throughout the whole of his earthly life to show us how it ought to be kept.

Therefore we need to remember the words of this hymn that allows us to remember the law in which God has written onto our hearts through Jesus Christ.
"My dear Redeemer and my Lord,
I read my duty in thy Word,
But in thy life the law appears
Drawn oat in living characters."

But, although we can read that law in the Scriptures, and see it wrought out in the life of Christ, yet we do need the Spirit of God come and enlighten us with regards to it, if we are really to know what it is.

Otherwise, a man and a woman may hear the Ten Commandments read every Sabbath day, and go on breaking them without ever knowing that he is breaking them; he may be keeping the letter of the commandments, and yet all the while be violating their spirit.

When the Holy Spirit comes to us, he shows us what the law really is. Take, for instance, the command, *"Thou shalt not commit adultery." "Well!"* says one, *"I have not broken that commandment." "Stay,"* says the Spirit of God, *"till you know the spiritual meaning of that command, for whosoever looketh on a woman to lust after her hath committed adultery with her already in his heart."*

There is, also, the command, *"Thou shalt not kill." "Oh!"* says the man, *"I never killed anybody, I have not committed murder." "But,"* says the Spirit of God, *"whosoever hateth his brother is a murderer."*

When the Lord thus writes his law upon our heart, he makes us know the far-reaching power and scope of the commandment. He causes us to understand that it touches not only actions and words, but thoughts, and the most transient imaginations, the things that are scarcely born within us, the sights that pass in a moment across the mind, like a stray passenger who passes in front of the camera when a photographer is taking a view.

The Spirit of God teaches us that even these momentary impressions are sinful, and that the very thought of foolishness is sin.

A question we need to ask ourselves is did we ever have truth truly written on our hearts?

If so, then you would have abhorred into thinking and saying, *"Who can stand before this terrible law? Who can ever hope to keep these commandments?"*

When we look to the flames that Moses saw on Mt Sinai; we can see that he had shrank and trembled almost unto despair, and then entreated that these terrible words should not be spoken to us any more.

Yet we could see that it was good and thus were made to know the law, not in the letter of it only, but in its cutting crushing, killing spirit for it work death to self-righteousness and death to all carnal boastings. When the law comes, sin revives, and we die; that is all that can come of it by itself.

Yet is it necessary that there should be such a death as that, and that there should be such a revival of sin that we may know the truth about it and under the force of that truth may be driven to the Lord Jesus Christ, who is the end of the Law for righteousness to every one that believeth.

Therefore, the writing of the law in our hearts means, first, makes us know what the law really is. If that is done, the Lord is pleased, then the next, is to cause his people to remember that law.

When a thing is "learnt by heart," we know the common meaning of that expression, even amongst our children.

If we have learnt a thing by heart rather than merely by rote, we have made it our own, and it remains with us. A man with whom God the Holy Spirit deals is one who does not have to go to the 20th of Exodus to know what the law is; he does not need to stop and ask concerning most things, *"Is this right?"* or, *"Is this wrong?"* but he carries within him a balance and a scale, a standard and test by which he can try these things for himself.

He has the law of his God written upon his heart, so that, almost as soon as he looks at a thing, he begins to perceive whether there is evil in it or whether it is good. There is a sort of sensitiveness in his soul which makes him discern between good and evil.

When God the Holy Spirit is dealing with him, there is a true, enlightened conscience within him, so that he no longer puts bitter for sweet and sweet for bitter, or darkness for light and light for darkness; but something within him tells him, *"This is right,"* or, *"That is wrong."*

It is a most blessed thing when this is the case, and it is always the work of the Spirit of God. There is some sort of a conscience in most men; in some it is a very small rush light, and that it is almost blown out by their evil habits. They can even make themselves think that they are doing right, when they are as wrong as wrong can be; but in a child of God there is a burning and a shining light which reveals the truth concerning sin.

There is within him a something that cannot be silenced; this is that principle or power which John Bunyan calls in his Holy War, *"Mr. Conscience the Recorder of Man soul." You know that, when the city of Man soul rebelled against the great King Shaddai, and came under the sway of Diabolus, they shut Mr. Recorder Conscience up in a dark room, for they did not want to let him see what was being done.*

Yet, notwithstanding, when the old gentleman had his fits, he used to sorely trouble the inhabitants of the guilty town, so they kept him under lock and key as much as possible.

But when Mr. Recorder Conscience gets full liberty, and lifts his brow into the sunlight, ah! Sirs, then are we guided in a very different way from that of ungodly men who follow their own evil course.

Then does the Lord say, "I will put my laws into their mind, and write them in their hearts."
The law is there to censure or to cheer; it is there to let us hear its voice say, "This is the way, walk ye in it;" or it is there to say, "Stay where you are, go no farther;" or, "Return, thou backsliding daughter, and seek mercy of the Lord."

God does more than that for his people. When he writes his law in our heart, he makes us to approve it.

An ungodly man wishes to alter God's law. *"There,"* says he, *"I do not like that command, 'Thou shalt not steal,' I should like to be a little bit of a trickster."*

Another says, *"I do not like that purity of which the minister spoke just now, I should like to indulge myself a little. Am I to have no pleasure?"*

But when the law of the Lord is written in his heart, the man says, *"The law is right."*

He would not alter it if he could; there is nothing that he hates more than the lowering of the tone of the law, for he does not want a lax morality. *"Oh, no!"* says he, *"let us have the highest form of righteousness that can be, and may God help me to live up to it!"*

Paul says, *"I delight in the law of God after the inward man;"* and so is it with every true child of God, he cannot think of the holiness of God without at once saying, *"I would not have him other than he is; let him be holy, holy, holy, Lord God of Sabbath, for as such I can worship him; but if he were less than that, I could not esteem him."*

If he hears of God's justice he delights even in that stern attribute, for he would not have an unjust God.

Is a great thing when God leads a man to approve of all that is right; I do not mean merely to acknowledge that it is right, but to be glad that it is so, and to wish that in his own soul he were conformed to it.

There is a further writing of the law in the heart when the man of God is made to appropriate that law, not only to approve of it, but to approve of it for himself.

There are many people who approve of laws as far as they keep their fellowmen in check, but they do not want laws for themselves. *"Oh!"* says such a person, *"of course, everybody ought to be honest; my servants ought not to peculate, they ought not to rob me, they ought to give me a good day's work for their wage."*

When the argument is turned round, and the question is about giving a good day's wage for the work, then they talk about political economy, which means that it is absolutely necessary that men should be dishonest. That is the pith and marrow of that political science, that every man will be selfish, and that there is no hope that people will be otherwise.

A man speaks that which is not true, and sees no evil in it; but if another should say anything against his character, that is a very different matter, it is quite unpardonable. He may walk through the earth, and devour men's characters as much as he pleases; that, of course, is mere criticism, such as we ought all to expect: but if he is touched, and there is a word spoken against him, it is cruel and unkind, and ought to be put down at once.

When God writes the law in a man's heart, he takes the law more to himself than he applies it to anybody else and his cry is not, *"See how my neighbours sin,"* but, *"See how I sin"*

His cry is not against his brother's, fault, but against his own fault. No longer does he look out for motes in other men s eyes, but he is most concerned about the beam which he is quite is in his own eye, he and prays the Lord to remove it.

However the law is not fully written in the heart till a man, approving the law and appropriating it to himself, feels he delights to obey it. *"There,"* he says, *"O my God, my highest happiness lies in doing as thou wouldst have me to do. I do not want any excuse or indulgence for sin, I want, above everything else, to be holy. It shall be my greatest pleasure to be pure; it shall be my perfect bliss to be perfectly holy. Thou hast so written thy law in my heart that, every time my heart beats, it seems to beat for holiness. Of my new-born nature are towards right, towards truth towards goodness, towards God."*

This is to have the law of the Lord written in our hearts so as to delight in it after the inward man, and to delight to practice it with the outward man, daily striving to make the entire life to be in accordance with the dictates of God's will.

Therefore is it not a wonderful thing that God shall ever make it as natural for us to be holy as once it was natural for us to be unholy, and that then we shall find it as much a joy to serve him as once we thought it a pleasure not to serve him, when, indeed, to deny ourselves shall cease to be self-denial?

It shall enjoyment to us to be nothing it shall be delight to renounce everything of self and to cling close to God, and to walk in his ways. Then will be fulfilled in our experience the promise of our text, I will put my laws into their mind, and write them in their hearts.

There is an old Latin proverb which says that "*things that are written remain;*" and I quote that proverb here believing that it is intended in the text to teach us that, when God's law is written in our hearts, it is retained there.

The lawyer always says, *"You had better be careful what you say, but when you go to law, never write anything, hold back from the use of pen and ink, for that what is written remains."*

When God writes his law in our hearts, he writes that which will never be blotted out. Once let him take the pen is hand. And begin to write. *"Holiness unto the Lord"* right across a man's heart and the devil himself can never remove that sacred line.

So it is meant, in our text as a part of the covenant, that God will write *"holiness"* so deeply upon the nature of his chosen people that they may sooner cease to be than cease to be holy. He will so put his law right into their hearts that we must tear their hearts out before we can tear out their conformity to the mind of God.

Is this not a wonderful method of writing the law in the heart?

This is sanctification indeed.

May God work it in each one of us! and he will if we are believers in the Lord Jesus Christ; for if we trust in Christ, we are in the covenant, and being in the covenant, this is the promise concerning us, *"I will put my laws into their mind, and write them in their hearts: and I will be to Thom a God, and they shall be to me a people."*

What does it mean by which this blessing is given?

It means the pens that God uses when he writes upon human hearts. First, God writes his law upon his people's hearts with the pen of gratitude. He tells them that Jesus Christ loves them, and gave himself for them. He gives them a sight of the bleeding Saviour, and tells them that their sin is put away by his death. Then, in return, they love the Lord with all their heart, and mind, and soul, and strength, the best way to make a man keep a law is to make him love the law-giver.

We thought at one time that God was a cruel tyrant, but we have learned that he is our loving Father. We could not have thought that he would have given his only-begotten Son to die as the Substitute for us; but, now that he has done so, we love him with all our heart.

There is one way of writing the law of God in our heart by giving us gratitude as the motive of a new life. The natural man's only motive for being good is, *"If I am good, I shall go to heaven; and if I am bad, I shall go to hell."*

That is the slave's motive; but the child of God is no more a slave, he has been delivered from his former bondage. He says, "*I am saved by sovereign grace, therefore I shall go to heaven. I shall never go to hell, which cannot be. I am God's chosen one, washed in the blood of the Lamb, and 'Now for the love I bear his name, What was my gain I count my loss; My former pride I call my shame, And nail my glory to his cross. Chosen, not for any goodness of my own, but entirely of the free and sovereign grace of God; tell me now what I can do to show my gratitude to such a gracious God."*

That is one way in which the law of the Lord gets written in the hearts of his people. Again, the law is written in the heart by repentance working hatred of sin.

Burnt children, are we afraid of the fire?

Oh, what a horror we have had sin ever since the day when we felt its power over our soul! It was enough to drive us mad when we felt the guilt of sin; it would have done so, I sometimes think, if I had continued much longer in that terrible condition.

O sin, sin, I have had enough of thee! Thus it didn’t ever bring me more than to a moment's seeming joy, and with it there came a deep and awful bitterness which burns within me to this day!

And now, being set free from sin, can I go back to it?

There are some that came to Christ with such difficulty that we were saved, as it were, by the skin of your teeth. We were like Jonah; you had to come up from the bottom of the mountains, and out of the very belly of hell where we cried unto God.

Well, that experience has made sin so bitter to us that we will not go back to it. The law has been written in our heart with the steel pen of repentance, and God has made sin to be a horrible evil to us.

Further more to that, the deeper than that God also writes his law upon the heart in regeneration, wherein he creates in man a new and better life. In regeneration, is born in us a new nature. Our old nature is all sin, and it will never be anything else but sin.

We may doctor it as we will, but it is a body of sin and death, and it will always remain so; but the new nature, which is born in us at our new birth, cannot sin, because it is born of God. It is a living and incorruptible seed, which lives and abides for ever; and that new heart, that right spirit, from its very birth, from its very origin, from its very nature, has the law and will of God engraved upon it.

To the new nature, it is as natural to obey as to the old nature it is natural to disobey. To the new nature, it is as much its element to live in holiness as to the old nature it is its element to live in sin.

Thus, by regeneration, the law of the Lord is written in the heart of his people. Again, God writes his law the more fully in the heart of his people as they increase in knowledge. The more we know of God, of this life, of the life to

Come, of heaven and hell, of the person of Christ, of the atonement, and of every other subject that is taught us in the Scriptures, the more we see the evil of sin, and the more we see the delights of holiness.

Why, at the very first moment of his conversion, man is afraid of sin because of what he has seen of it; but as he begins to perceive how sin put the Christ to death, how sin digged the pit of hell, how sin brought all the plagues and curses upon the human family, and will continue to curse generations yet unborn, then the man says, *"How can I do this great wickedness, and sin against God?"* Trained and educated in the school of Christ, the more he knows, the more he delights in the law and the will of God.

And thus, the law is written in the heart, as God makes the new life in us to grow and increase. There are some Christians, which have but little spiritual life. There is a story there a man of God who has been preaching the gospel in the New Hebrides, where till lately the people were cannibals; and, by God's grace, he has brought hundreds, if not thousands, of the former savages to become Christians; and the good brother, when he spoke of his hardships, said, *"All, but you do not know in England the joys of those who preach to cannibals!"*

This is true, most of the early missionaries who first went out to preach and help the people were killed and eaten, and our friend escaped by the skin of his teeth; Yet the preacher when asked what his special and peculiar joys were. *"Oh!"* he said, "*the joy of converting a cannibal to Christ is a greater bliss than can be known by you, who only bring ordinary people to the Saviour; and,"* he added, *"I tell you that there are no Christians that I know of that excel my converted cannibals. If you want to see the Sabbath day sacredly kept, you must come into my place, and see how these people who used to be cannibals keep it. Those who were accustomed to eat their fellow-men, now never rise without prayer, and never sit at the table without asking a blessing.*

There is not a Christian household but has family prayer in it, morning and evening. These people walk with God," said the missionary, "and live close to Christ; and as I look at them, it seems such a joy to have been the means of bringing these cannibals to Christ."

However there are many nominally Christian people who are not half as good as those converted cannibals.

What is the reason?

It is because they seem to have God's life poured into them abundantly, and some among us have but little of it. Now, when a man gets the life of God abundantly poured into him, he is sensitive against sin, for he has the law of God written in his heart, and thereby God has made his conscience; *"Quick as the apple of an eye."*

He cannot bear to hear an ill word from others, or himself have an evil thought without being grieved and troubled. There are men and women who have professed to be Christians do many questionable things, and yet never feel that they were doing any wrong; but as for the true Christian, who lives near to God, and who has been acting perfectly right as far as other people could judge, when he gets home, he begins blaming himself for something he did not do.

As far as we can see, he has said and done the right thing; but he says, *"No, I did not say it as earnestly as I ought to have said it; I did not do it as I ought to have done it."*

When we look to ourselves and question do we live near to God and keep his laws. As for myself, I know that, when I live near to God, I am most conscious of sin; and I believe that, in proportion as we get away from God, we then begin to think that we are perfect; but if we live in the light of the Lord, sin will be a daily plague to us, and we will be crying for the precious blood to wash us.

It is the man who is spiritually blind who talks about his holiness, but it is the one whose eyes have been opened of God, the really holy man whom God has brought near to himself, who still cries out,
"Holier! Holier! Higher."
"Nearer, my God, to thee,
Nearer to thee!
Even though it is a cross that raised me.
Still all my song shall be.
Nearer, my God, to thee!
Nearer to thee!"

And this is how God writes his law in his people's hearts, by giving them so much light that they become tender and sensitive at the very approach of sin. And, once more, communing with Christ is the best way of getting the law written in the heart.

He who is with Christ from morning to noon, and from noon to dewy eve, and who can say at night,
"Sprinkled afresh with pardoning blood,
I lay me down to rest,
As in the embraces of my God,
Or on my Saviour's breast,"

He is the man who will have the law of God written in his heart. The questions in which one may ask:

How can he sin whose garments smell of the myrrh and aloes and cassia of communion with Christ?

How can he come out of the ivory palaces of fellowship with his Lord, and then go and live as others do, and sin against his God?

The answer is that the Lord writes his law in the hearts of his people.

What is meant by the great grace which is contained in this blessing?

There is not a greater gift than this that even God can bestow, except the gift of his only-begotten

Son: *"I will put my laws into their mind, and write them in their hearts."*

As sinners we are to keep the law; but, without the Spirit of God working within us, nothing will come of it!

But if God puts his law into our hearts, then we will keep it. Oh, that he might even now lead us to his dear Son, which we might see his law in the hand of Christ, and then feel that pierced hand dropping it into our heart to abide there for ever!

The great grace of this blessing lies here.

First, God does what man would not and could not do. Man would not keep the law, he refused to obey it; so God comes, in the splendour of his grace, and changes his will, renews his heart, alters his affections, so that, what man would not do, God does.

Man has also become so fallen that he cannot keep the law. Sooner might the Ethiopian change his skin, or the leopard his spots, than h that is accustomed to do evil learn to do well; but what man cannot do, by reason of the perversity of the flesh, God performs within him, working in him to will and to do of his good pleasure.

Oh, what amazing grace is this, which while it forgives our want of will, also removes our want of power!

Is this not a wonderful proof of grace that God does this without destroying man in any degree whatever?

Man is a creature with a will, a *"free will"* a creature that is responsible for his actions; so God does not come and change our hearts by a physical process, as some seem to dream, but by a spiritual process in which he never mars our nature, but sets our nature right.

If a man becomes a child of God, he still has a will. God does not destroy the delicate machinery of our nature, but he puts it into proper gear. We become Christians with our own full assent and consent; and we keep the law of God not by any compulsion except the sweet compulsion of love.

We do not keep it because we cannot do otherwise, but we keep it because we would not do otherwise, because we have come to delight therein, and this seems to me the greatest wonder of divine grace.

Therefore we can now see how different the Lord's way of working and ours is. If we knock down a man who is living an evil life, and put him in chains, we can make him honest by force; or if we set him free, and hem him round with Acts of Parliament, we may make him sober if he cannot get anything to drink, we may make him wonderfully quiet if you put a gag in his mouth; but that is not God's way of acting.

He who put man in the Garden of Eden, and never put any palisades around the tree of the knowledge of good and evil, but left man a free agent, does just the same in the operations of his grace. He leaves his people to the influences that are within them, and yet they go right, because they are so changed and renewed by his grace that they delight to do that which once they loathed to do.

We are to admire the grace of God in his actions. We should have taken tile watch to pieces, and broken half the wheels, and made new ones, or something of the kind. But God knows how to leave the man just as much a man as he was before his conversion, and yet to make him so entirely a new man that old things have passed away, and all things have become new. And this is very beautiful, too, that when God writes his law in his people's hearts, He makes this the way of their preservation.

When God's law is written in a man's heart, which heart becomes divinely royal property, for the King's name is there, and the heart in which God has written his name can never perish. Now, when the Lord once writes his name in your heart, he writes his law within you; and though the devil may batter you, God will claim you as his own.

Temptation and sin may assail you, but if the law of the Lord is in our heart, we shall not give way to sin, we shall resist it, we shall be preserved, we shall be kept, for you are the Lord's. This is the only way of salvation that I know of for all of us.

First, we must be washed in the fountain filled with blood; and next, we must have the law of God written in our inward parts. Then shall we be safe beyond fear of ruin. *"They shall be mine,"* saith the Lord of hosts, *"in that day when I make up my jewels."*

Oh, blessed plan of salvation!

May it be accepted by every man and woman!

And it can only be so by the work of the Spirit of God leading us to a simple trust in the Lord Jesus Christ. Trust Christ to save us, and he will do it, as surely as he is the Christ of God. God help us to trust him now! Amen.

Jeremiah 31:27-37; *"Behold, the days come, saith the Lord, that I will sow the house of Israel and the house of Judah with the seed of man, and with the seed of beast. And it shall come to pass, that like as I have watched over them, to pluck up, and to break down, and to throw down, and to destroy, and to afflict; so will I watch over them, to build, and replant, saith the Lord. In those days they shall say no more, The fathers have eaten a sour grape, and the children's teeth are set on edge.*
But every one shall die for his own iniquity: every man that eateth the sour grapes, his teeth shall be set on edge. Behold, the days come, saith the Lord, that I will make a new covenant with the house of Israel, and with the house of Judah: not according to the covenant that I made with their fathers in the day that I took them by the hand to bring them out of the land of Egypt; which my covenant they brake, although I was an husband unto them, saith the Lord: but this shall be the covenant that I will make with the house of Israel; After those days, saith the Lord, I will put my law in their inward parts, and write it in their hearts; and will be their God, and they shall be my people."

This is the central truth of all Scripture; it is the basis of all Scripture. When Paul desires to set forth the covenant of grace, he appeals to this passage. Twice, in the book of Hebrews, he bases an argument upon it, and after quoting it, adds, *"Whereof the Holy Ghost also is a witness to us."*

We can see that under the first covenant we are ruined; there is no salvation for us but under this new covenant, wherefore let us read to our joy and comfort what the promises and provisions of that new covenant are.

Jeremiah 31:34; *"And they shall teach no more every man his neighbour, and every man his brother, saying, Know the LORD: for they shall all know me, from the least of them unto the greatest of them, saith the LORD: for I will forgive their iniquity, and I will remember their sin no more."*

Pardoned sin, as well as the change of nature, is implied in the writing of the law upon the heart.

Oh, what a privilege it is to be among these covenanted people!

How shall we know whether we belong to them?

The seal of the covenant is faith in Christ; it is the personal seal upon the heart and conscience. Those who believe in Jesus Christ as our Saviour, those who are trusting alone to his stoning sacrifice, then God is in covenant with us, for Jesus is the Mediator of the new covenant, and he who has Christ has the Surety of the covenant, and he shall have in due time every blessing which that covenant guarantees.

Jeremiah 31:35-37; *"Thus saith the LORD, which giveth the sun for a light by day, and the ordinances of the moon and of the stars for a light by night, which divideth the sea when the waves thereof roar; The LORD of hosts is his name: if those ordinances depart from before me, saith the LORD, then the seed of Israel also shall cease from being a nation before me for ever.*

Thus saith the LORD; If heaven above can be measured, and the foundations of the earth searched out beneath, I will also cast off all the seed of Israel for all that they have done, saith the LORD."

Now Israel still stands as a people separate from all others, and there is still before the literal seed of Israel a great and glorious future; but as for the spiritual Israel, who worship God in the Spirit, and have no confidence in the flesh, God will sooner blot out the sun and moon than cast away his people, or any one of them.

They shall all be his people, and he shall be their God; he will preserve them, and he will keep his covenant with them for ever and for ever, blessed be his holy name, the name of Jehovah, the God of the covenant which cannot be broken!

Importance of the Law and Gospel

This chapter looks at the importance of the Law and Gospel in the hope that it will enable us to understand further what God is saying.

Why is the subject of "law and gospel" important?

There are six reasons to why the subject of the law and gospel are important. Yet there are many Christians who make a lot of mistakes as they do not understand the proper relationship which exists between the law and the gospel.

The bible tells us there can be no true evangelical holiness, either in heart or life, except it proceed from faith working by love; and no true faith, either of the law or the gospel, unless the leading distinction between the one and the other are spiritually discerned.

The law and the gospel are set before us in the Bible as one undivided system of truth, yet an unchangeable line of distinction is drawn between them. There is also an inseparable connection and relationship.

There are unfortunately some Christians who see the difference between them but not the relationship; however, the man who knows the relative position of the law and the gospel has the keys of the situation in understanding the Bible and its doctrine.

A proper understanding between the law and the gospel is the mark of a Christian who rightly divides the word of truth. Even true ministers of God rightly divide the word of truth.

Charles Bridges summed up this mark of a true minister and Christian: "*The mark of a minister `approved unto God, a workman that needeth not to be ashamed', is, that he `rightly divides the word of truth.' This implies a full and direct application of the gospel to the mass of his unconverted hearers, combines with a body of spiritual instruction to the several classes of Christians.*

His system will be marked by Scriptural symmetry and comprehensiveness. It will embrace the whole revelation of God, in its doctrinal instructions, experimental privileges and practical results. This revelation is divided into two parts--the Law and the Gospel--essentially distinct from each other; though so intimately connected, that no accurate knowledge of either can be obtained without the other...." (The Christian Ministry, London: Banner of Truth Trust, 1967, p. 222).

The law, like Christ, has always been crucified between two thieves Antinomianism on the one side and Legalism on the other side.

What is antinomian?

In short antinomian sees no relationship between the law and the gospel except that of being free. However in the New Testament Paul of Tarsus, in his Letters, claims several times that believers are saved by the unearned grace of God, not by good works, "lest anyone should boast", and placed a priority on orthodoxy (right belief) before orthopraxy (right practice).

Paul's statements on this matter have always been a matter of dispute by many Christians and ministers.

In 2 Peter 3:16; *"As also in all his letters, speaking in them concerning these things, in which are some things hard to understand, which the unlearned and unsteadfast twist, as also the remaining Scriptures, to their own destruction."*

The ancient Gnostics interpreted Paul to be referring to the manner in which embarking on a path to enlightenment ultimately leads to enlightenment, which was their idea of what constituted salvation. However, this is interpreted as a reference to salvation simply by trusting Christ.

Paul used the term freedom in Christ; Galatians 2:4; *"And because of false brothers brought in unawares, who came in alongside to spy out our liberty which we have in Christ Jesus, that they might bring us into servitude,"*

It is clear that some Christians have understood this to mean lawlessness (i.e. not obeying Mosaic Law).

Yet in Acts 18:12-16; *"And Gallio being proconsul of Achaia, the Jews rushed with one passion against Paul, and led him to the judgment seat,*
13 Saying that, He incites men to worship God contrary to the law.
14 And Paul being about to open his mouth, Gallio said to the Jews, If indeed therefore it were a wrong or reckless act, Oh you Jews, I would hold up myself according to reason with you,
15 But if it is a question about words and names and of law according to you, you will see to it yourselves, because I will absolutely not to be judge of these things.
16 And he pushed them from the judgment seat."

We can see here that Paul is accused of *"persuading ... People to worship God in ways contrary to the law."*

In Acts 21:21; *"And they are catechized concerning you, that you teach standing away from Moses to all the Jews who are among the races, saying not to circumcise their children, and not to walk after the customs."*

Colossians 2:13-14; *"And you, being dead in your transgressions, and the uncircumcision of your flesh, he has made alive together with him, having graced to you all the transgressions, Wiping out the handwriting of the decrees contrary to us, and lifted it out of the midst, nailing it to the cross."*

Some would see this as proof of Paul's antinomistic views.

However, within the context of the following verses, especially verse Colossians 2:16; *"Therefore do not let anyone judge you in food, or in drink,or in sharing of a festival, or a new moon festival, or of the Sabbaths,"*

Where Paul states that current behaviour is also free from "judgement", it appears more likely that Paul, or whoever wrote Colossians, is claiming the Law itself has been abolished.

Yet, all of these are festivals from the Law of Moses. This verse in no way gives believers permission to attend idolatrous festivals. Paul's instructions are that believers (Hebrews or ethnics) could participate or not participate in Mosaic festivals, and were not to be judged by other believers who did or by believers who did not.

The Sabbath is the only Commandment of the Ten that is not restated in the New Covenant as binding upon Christian believers. God will bless any believer who observes the Sabbath for the right heart reasons, but no one must make Sabbath (Saturday) or Sunday observance a condition of salvation or even of complete obedience to God.

We are not to forsake the assembling of ourselves together for public worship of God, and the preaching of the good news of His Son, Heb 10:25; *"Not forsaking the assembling of ourselves together, as the habit of some, but comforting, and so much the more, as you see the day drawing near,"*

However, there is nothing in the New Covenant that says a believer who goes to church services on Sunday is more obedient than a believer who attends church services on another day or night.

The Sabbath was definitely not included by the Apostles in their instructions in Acts 15, *"And some men going down from Judaea taught the brothers that, If you are not circumcised after the custom of Moses, you absolutely do not have power to be saved.*
2 There being therefore by Paul and Barnabas absolutely no small uprising and dispute with them, they ordained for Paul and Barnabas, and some others of them, to go up to Jerusalem to the apostles and elders about this debate.
3 They indeed therefore being sent forward by the church, went through Phenice and Samaria, narrating fully the conversion of the races, and they made great joy to all the brothers.
4 And having come into Jerusalem, they were welcomed by the church and the apostles and elders, and announced what things God did with them.
5 And some from the party of the Pharisees who believed, stood up saying that it was necessary to circumcise them, also to command them to keep the Law of Moses.
6 Also the apostles and elders came together to see about this word.
7 And there being much mutual questioning, Peter standing up, said to them, Men, brothers, you know that from the first days God chose among us for the other races to hear the word of the good news through my mouth, and believe.
8 And God, the heart knower, witnessed to them, giving them the Holy Spirit, just as to us,
9 And absolutely did not discriminate between both us and them, purifying their hearts by faith.
10 Now therefore why do you tempt God, to impose a yoke upon the neck of the disciples, which absolutely neither our fathers nor we had strength to lift?
11 But through the grace of the Lord Jesus Christ we believe we shall be saved, according to the same manner as they.
12 And all the multitude kept silence, and heard Barnabas and Paul bringing out what signs and wonders God had done among the races through them.
13 And after their silence, James answered, saying, Men, brothers, hear me.
14 Simeon has brought out how God at first visited to take out of the races a people for his name.
15 And to this agree the words of the prophets, as it has been written,
16 After these things I will conduct myself back, and will build again the tent of David which has fallen, and I will build again its ruins, and I will set it upright,
17 So that the rest of men may seek out the Lord, even all the races upon whom my name is called, says the Lord, who is doing all these things.
18 Known to God from eternity are all his works.
19 Therefore I judge not to cause trouble for those turning to God from the other races;
20 But to write to them, that they abstain from defilements of idols, and from sexual promiscuity, and from things strangled, and blood,
21 Because Moses from ancient generations has in every city those preaching him, being read in the synagogues every Sabbath.
22 Then it was the opinion of the apostles and elders, with the whole church, to send chosen men of themselves to Antioch with Paul and Barnabas, namely, Judas surnamed Barsabas, and Silas, governing men among the brothers,
23 Writing through their hand these things: The apostles and elders, and brothers, to those throughout Antioch, and Syria, and Cilicia, brothers out of the races, greeting:
24 Since we heard that some of us having gone out stirred you with words, upsetting your souls,

saying, Be circumcised and keep the law, which we absolutely did not so charge,
25 It was our thought, being assembled with one passion, to send chosen men to you with our beloved Barnabas and Paul, Men who have given their souls over to the name of our Lord Jesus Christ.
27 We have therefore set apart and sent Judas and Silas who will also announce the same things by mouth,
28 Because it was the thought of the Holy Spirit, and us, to impose upon you no more weight than these necessary things:
29 That you abstain from things offered to idols, and from blood, and from things strangled, and from sexual promiscuity, out of which guarding yourselves completely, you are practicing good. Be in health.
30 Therefore indeed being set free, they came to Antioch, and gathering the multitude together, they delivered the written message;
31 And having read it, they rejoiced upon the comfort.
32 And Judas and Silas, also being themselves prophets, exhorted the brothers with many words, and confirmed them.
33 And having continued a time, they were set free with peace from the brothers to the apostles.
34 And Silas thought for himself to remain.
35 And Paul and Barnabas continued in Antioch, teaching and announcing the good news, also many others.
36 And after some days Paul said to Barnabas, Indeed, having turned back, let us watch over our brothers throughout every city in which we have preached the word of the Lord, how they are holding.
37 And Barnabas determined to take along with them John called Mark.
38 And Paul deemed it not fit to take him with them, he having removed himself from them from Pamphylia, and did not go with them into the work.
39 Therefore there became a sharp feeling, so as to split them one from the other, and having taken Mark along, Barnabas sailed away into Cyprus;
40 And Paul having chosen Silas, went out, being given over to the grace of God by the brothers.
41 And he went through Syria and Cilicia, confirming the churches."

And here in Paul's writings is the only place it is dealt with in any of the apostolic writings.

Romans 10:4; *"Because Christ is the end of the law into righteousness to everyone who believes,"*

This verse means that Christ is the Law and we are led into righteousness all who believe and accept him as Lord and saviour.

Ephesians 2:15; *"In his flesh having rendered inoperative the hostility, the law of commandments in decrees, in order to create of the two in himself one new man, making peace;"*

Paul also wrote or spoke in support of the law,

Romans 2:12–16, *"Because as many as have sinned without law will also be destroyed without law, and as many as have sinned in the law will be judged through the law,*
13 Because absolutely not the hearers of the law are righteous with God, but the doers of the law are made righteous,
14 Because when the races, not having the law, do by nature the things of the law, these, not having the law, are a law to themselves,
15 Who show the work of the law written in their hearts, their conscience witnessing with them, and their calculations between one another formally charging them or else defending them,
16 In the day when God will judge the secrets of men by Jesus Christ according to my good news."

Romans 3:31, *"Therefore do we render the law inoperative through faith? We do not! On the contrary, we cause the law to stand."*

Romans 7:12, *"Therefore truly the law is holy, and the commandment holy, and righteous, and inherently good."*

Romans 8:7–8, *"On this very account the fleshly mind is hostile against God, because it absolutely will not arrange itself under the law of God, because it absolutely does not have the power. And those being in the flesh absolutely do not have the power to please God."*

Galatians 5:3, *"And I testify again to every man being circumcised, that he is a debtor to do the whole law"*

Acts 24:14, *"But this I confess to you, that according to the way which they call a party, so I officially minister to the God of my fathers, believing all things according to the written law and prophets;"*

Acts 25:8; *"Defending himself, he said, Absolutely not against the law of the Jews, and absolutely not against the temple, and absolutely not against Caesar, have I sinned anything."*

Paul also preached about Ten Commandment topics such as idolatry etc:

1 Corinthians 5:11, *"But now I have written to you not to mix with, if anyone that is called a brother is a fornicator, or covetous, or an idolater, or is abusive, or a drunkard, or an extortioner; with this sort do not eat,"*

1 Corinthians 6:9–10, *"Or do you absolutely not see that the unrighteous will not inherit the kingdom of God? Do not be led astray; absolutely no fornicators, absolutely no idolaters, absolutely no adulterers, absolutely no effeminate, absolutely no homosexuals, Absolutely no thieves, absolutely no covetous, absolutely no drunkards, absolutely no revilers, absolutely no extortioners, will inherit the kingdom of God."*

1 Corinthians 10:7, *"Neither be idolaters, as some of them, as it has been written, The people sat down to eat and drink, and stood up to play."*

1 Corinthians 10:14, *"Therefore, my dearly beloved, run from idolatry."*

Galatians 5:19–21, *"And the works of the flesh are manifest, which are: Adultery, sexual promiscuity, uncleanness, lack of moral restraint,*
20 Idolatry, use of drugs, hatred, quarrelling, jealousies, hard breathing, strife, dissensions, heresies,
21 Envyings, murders, drunkenness, carousings, and the such like, which I tell you before, as I also said previously, that those practicing such things will absolutely not inherit the kingdom of God."

Ephesians 5:5, *"Because be knowing this, that every fornicator, or unclean one, or covetous one, who is an idolater, has absolutely no inheritance in the kingdom of Christ and of God."*

Colossians 3:5, *"Put to death therefore your members which are upon the earth: sexual promiscuity, uncleanness, passions, worthless longings, and covetousness, which is idolatry,"*

Acts 17:16–21, *"And awaiting them in Athens, Paul's spirit was sharpened in him, looking with special interest at the city being totally idolatrous.*

17 Therefore indeed he spoke thoroughly in the synagogue with the Jews and with those worshipping, also in the market during every day with those who happened to be there.
18 And some of the Epicureans and the Stoics, philosophers, fell in with him. And some said, What does this seed-picker will to say? And the others, He seems to be a preacher of foreign demons, because he announced to them the good news of Jesus and the resurrection.
19 Also taking hold upon him, they led him upon the Areos Pagus, saying, May we have power to know what is this new teaching you are speaking?
20 Because you carry some foreign things into our hearing; we are determined therefore to know what you will these things to be.
21 (And all the Athenians and foreigners residing there had a good time in absolutely nothing else, but either to speak something, or to hear new things.)"

Acts 19:23–41; *"And there was at that time absolutely no small disturbance concerning that way,*
24 Because one named Demetrius, a silversmith, making silver shrines of Artemis, afforded the craftsmen absolutely no small trade;
25 Also whom assembling together the workmen of such things, said, Men, you know that out of this trade is our wealth.
26 Also you look with special interest and hear that absolutely not only in Ephesus, but almost in all of Asia, this Paul convincing, has transferred an ample crowd, saying that there are absolutely no gods caused to exist by hands;
27 And absolutely not only is this our part in danger of coming into disrepute, but also that the temple of the great goddess Artemis will be accounted as absolutely nothing, and her glorious splendour is about to be destroyed, whom all Asia and the inhabited earth worships.
28 And hearing this, becoming full of hard breathing, they screamed, saying, Great is Artemis of the Ephesians.
29 And the city being filled with a riotous disturbance, they rushed violently with one passion into the theatre, having seized Gaius and Aristarchus, men of Macedonia, Paul's companions in travel.
30 And Paul intending to go into the people, the disciples absolutely did not let him.
31 And some of the presidents of the public festivities of Asia, being his friends, sent to him, calling on him not to give himself into the theatre.
32 Then others screamed one thing, and some another, because the assembly was thrown into disorder, and the majority absolutely did not see why they were convened.
33 And they drove Alexander out of the multitude, the Jews pushing him forward. And Alexander motioning downward with the hand, determined to make his defence to the public.
34 And recognizing that he was a Jew, there became one voice out of all for over two hours screaming, Great is Artemis of the Ephesians.
35 And the town-clerk settling down the multitude, said, Men of Ephesus, for what man is there who absolutely does not know that the city of the Ephesians is a temple keeper of the great goddess Artemis, and of the one fallen from Zeus?
36 Therefore these things being indisputable, it is necessary that you become settled down and practice nothing rashly,
37 Because you have brought these men, who are absolutely neither templerobbers nor blasphemers of your goddess.
38 Therefore if indeed Demetrius and those craftsmen with him have a word against anyone, the courts are available, and there are proconsuls; let them accuse one another.
39 But if you inquire to take away any other things, it shall be solved in a lawful assembly,
40 Because we also are in danger of being accused of an insurrection concerning today, there existing not even one legal cause by which we have power to give a word for this riotous crowd.
41 And having spoken these things, he set the assembly free."

We can see that Paul did not object to the observance of the Mosaic Law, as long as it did not interfere with the liberty of the Gentiles, but he conformed to it on occasions when required.

1 Corinthians 9:20; *"And I became to the Jews as a Jew, that I might gain Jews; to those under law, as under law, that I might gain those under law;"*

Thus shortly after the Council of Jerusalem circumcised Timothy Acts 16:1-
3, *"And he arrived into Derbe and Lystra, and behold, a certain disciple was there, named Timothy, the son of a certain faithful Jewish woman, and his father a Greek,*
2 Who had a good testimony among the brothers at Lystra and Iconium.
3 Paul determined for him to go out with him, and taking him, circumcised him because of the Jews being in those places, because they all saw that his father was a Greek."

We can see that Paul was observing the Mosaic ritual when he was arrested at Jerusalem. Many people have been led to believe that Paul was to convert only the Gentiles to the seven moral laws of Noah and to let the Jews follow the Mosaic Law, which explains the apparent contradictions in the New Testament regarding the laws of Moses and the Sabbath.

At the time historians have led us to believe that there was a conflict between Paul Christianity and the Jerusalem Church led by James the Just, Simon Peter, and John the Apostle, the so-called "Jewish Christians" or Pillars of the Church.

Yet we can see that in the bible Paul writes that he was an observant Jew, and that Christians should *"uphold the Law"*

Romans 3:31; *"Therefore do we render the law inoperative through faith? We do not! On the contrary, we cause the law to stand."*

In Galatians 2:14, *"But when I saw that they absolutely did not walk uprightly with the truth of the good news, I said to Peter in front of all, If you, being a Jew, live as one of another race, and absolutely not as Jews, why do you constrain the races to be Jews?"*

We can see that this was a part of the *"Incident at Antioch."* Where Paul publicly accused Peter of judaizing. Even so, he does go on to say that sins remain sins, and upholds by several examples the kind of behaviour that the church should not tolerate.

Galatians 5:19-21, *"And the works of the flesh are manifest, which are: Adultery, sexual promiscuity, uncleanness, lack of moral restraint,*
20 Idolatry, use of drugs, hatred, quarrelling, jealousies, hard breathing, strife, dissensions, heresies,
21 Envyings, murders, drunkenness, carousings, and the such like, which I tell you before, as I also said previously, that those practicing such things will absolutely not inherit the kingdom of God."

1 Corinthians 6:9-10; *"Or do you absolutely not see that the unrighteous will not inherit the kingdom of God? Do not be led astray; absolutely no fornicators, absolutely no idolaters, absolutely no adulterers, absolutely no effeminate, absolutely no homosexuals, Absolutely no thieves, absolutely no covetous, absolutely no drunkards, absolutely no revilers, absolutely no extortioners, will inherit the kingdom of God."*

In 1 Corinthians 7:10-16; *"And to those having married I charge, absolutely not I, but the Lord, Do not let the wife be separated from her husband;*
11 And if she indeed is separated, let her remain unmarried, or be reconciled to her husband; and

do not let the husband leave his wife.
12 And to the rest I speak, absolutely not the Lord: If any brother has a wife who does not believe, and she thinks it good to be housed with him, do not let him send her away.
13 And if any woman has a husband who does not believe, and if he thinks it good to be housed with her, do not let her send the man away,
14 Because the unbelieving husband is sanctified in the wife, and the unbelieving wife is sanctified in the husband, else then your children are unclean, but now they are holy.
15 And if the unbelieving separates, let him separate; a brother or a sister is absolutely not under bondage in such matters, and God has called us to peace,
16 Because what do you see, wife, if you will save your husband? Or what do you see husband, if you will save your wife?"

Paul reiterating Jesus' teaching on divorce "not I but the Lord" and does not reject it, but goes on to proclaim his own teaching "I, not the Lord", an extended counsel regarding a specific situation which some interpret as not in conflict with what the Lord said.

However, this may mean he received direct knowledge of what the Lord wanted him to teach through the Holy Ghost.

Galatians 2:6-10; *"And from these who were thought to be somewhat, whatever they were, it is absolutely of no surpassing importance to me; God absolutely does not take the face of man, because those thought to be somewhat conferred absolutely nothing to me;*
7 But on the contrary, seeing that I have been entrusted with the good news to the uncircumcision, as to Peter the circumcision,
8 Because the one supernaturally working in Peter to the apostleship of the circumcision, was supernaturally working in me to the races;
9 And James, Cephas, and John, those thought to be pillars, knowing the grace given to me, gave to me and Barnabas the right hands of partnership, that we go to the races, and they to the circumcision,
10 Only that we remember the poor, which also I exerted earnest speed to do this same thing."

James, in contrast, to Paul states that we are to obey the Law of God, that a person is justified by what he does and not by faith alone, that faith without works is dead,

James 2:14–26; *"What does it profit, my brothers, if anyone says he has faith, and does not have works? Faith does not have power to save him!*
15 If a brother or sister is naked, and lacks daily nourishment,
16 And one of you says to them, Go away in peace, be warmed and filled, and you do not give them the things needful for the body, what is the profit?
17 In this way, faith, if it does not have works, by itself is dead.
18 But, someone may speak, You have faith, and I have works. Show me your faith apart from your works, and I will show you my faith out of my works.
19 You believe that there is one God; you do beautifully well; the demons also believe and tremble.
20 And are you willing to know, Oh vain man, that faith apart from works is dead?
21 Was Abraham our father absolutely not justified out of works, having offered up Isaac his son upon the altar?
22 You see that faith worked with his works, and by the works faith was perfected.
23 And the Scripture was fulfilled saying, And Abraham believed God, and it was calculated to him for righteousness, and he was called Friend of God.
24 You see then that out of works a man is justified, and absolutely not out of faith only.
25 And similarly was Rahab the harlot absolutely not justified out of works, having received the messengers as her guests, and sending them out another way?

26 Because as the body apart from the spirit is dead, so also faith apart from works is dead."

It speaks that faith in Jesus Christ is the first step and that faith is justified through good works, he goes on to say that without spreading your love and faith, it is dead. Works are the evidence of faith. It's not faith and works; it's faith that works.

James 2:20; *"And are you willing to know, Oh vain man, that faith apart from works is dead?"*

Romans 2:6, *"Who will give back to everyone according to his deeds,"*

Ephesians 2:8-10, *"Because by grace you are saved, through faith, and that absolutely not out of yourselves; it is the gift of God,*
9 Absolutely not out of works, so that no one should boast,
10 Because we are his workmanship, created in Christ Jesus upon inherent good works, which God has prepared beforehand so that we should walk in them."

However, in the Gospel of Matthew Jesus called for full adherence to the commandments where in Matthew 5:19-21 He declared: *"Whoever therefore will make one of these least commandments loose, and teaches men in this way, he shall be called the least in the kingdom of heaven, and whoever does and teaches them, this one will be called great in the kingdom of heaven.*
20 Because I say to you that, Unless your righteousness shall excel in superiority that of the scribes and Pharisees, you shall absolutely not enter into the kingdom of heaven.
21 You heard that it has been spoken to the ancients, Absolutely do not murder, and whoever murders shall be liable in the judgment;"

Therefore we must remember that in 1 John 3:4 states: *"Everyone doing sin also does lawlessness, and sin is lawlessness."*

What is legalism?

Legalism as defined in the Wikipedia online encyclopaedia is a *"pejorative term referring to an improper fixation on law or codes of conduct, or legal ideas, usually implying an allegation of misguided rigor, pride, superficiality, the neglect of mercy, and ignorance of the grace of God or emphasizing the letter of law over the spirit.*
Legalism is alleged against any view that law, not faith in God's grace, is the pre-eminent principle of redemption. Its opposite error is antinomianism, which is alleged against a view that moral laws are not binding."

The legalist fails to understand that vital distinction between the two. However in the New Testament Jesus directed some of his harshest words at the Pharisees and their accompanying "scribes" and "lawyers," the guardians of the ritual law of Judaism.

Matthew 23; *"Then Jesus spoke to the crowd and to his disciples,*
2 Saying, The scribes and the Pharisees sit upon Moses' seat;
3 All things therefore whatever they say to you to keep, keep and do, and do not do according to their works, because they say, and absolutely do not do,
4 Because they bind heavy tasks and hard to lift, and lay them on men's shoulders, but they themselves absolutely will not to move them with one of their fingers.
5 And they do all their works to be looked at by men, and they enlarge their phylacteries, and magnify the fringes of their garments,
6 And love the first couch in the dinners, and the first seats in the synagogues,
7 And the greetings in the markets, and to be called by men, Rabbi, Rabbi.

8 And you do not be called Rabbi by men, because one is your Teacher, the Christ, and all you are brothers.
9 And do not call anyone your father upon the earth, because he is your Father, the one in heaven.
10 Neither be called Guides, because one is your Guide, the Christ.
11 And he who is greatest among you, let him be your minister.
12 And whoever will exalt himself shall be humbled, and whoever will humble himself shall be exalted.
13 And woe to you, scribes and Pharisees, hypocrites, because you shut the kingdom of heaven in front of men, because you absolutely do not go in, and you absolutely do not allow those going in to go in.
14 Woe to you, scribes and Pharisees, hypocrites, because you eat down widows' houses, and for a pretext are long praying; because of this you will receive super-abundant judgment.
15 Woe to you, scribes and Pharisees, hypocrites, because you go around sea and dry land to make one proselyte, and when he becomes one, you make him a child of hell twice more than yourselves.
16 Woe to you, blind guides, the ones saying, Whoever swears by the temple, it is absolutely nothing, but whoever swears by the gold of the temple, he is under obligation!
17 Fools and blind; because what is greater, the gold, or the temple sanctifying the gold?
18 And, Whoever swears by the altar, it is nothing, but whoever swears by the gift upon it is under obligation.
19 Fools and blind, because what is greater, the gift, or the altar sanctifying the gift?
20 The one therefore swearing by the altar, swears by it and by all things upon it.
21 And the one swearing by the temple, swears by it, and by the one permanently housed in it.
22 And the one swearing by heaven, swears by the throne of God, and by the one sitting upon it.
23 Woe to you, scribes and Pharisees, hypocrites, because you tithe mint, and dill, and cumin, and have left off the weightier matters of the law, judgment, and mercy, and faith; these things you need to do, and not to leave off those others.
24 Blind guides, the ones straining at a gnat and gulping down a camel!
25 Woe to you, scribes and Pharisees, hypocrites, because you cleanse the outside of the cup and of the dish, but inside they are full of pillage and lack of self-control.
26 Blind Pharisee, cleanse first the inside of the cup and of the dish, that the outside of them may be clean also.
27 Woe to you, scribes and Pharisees, hypocrites, because you are like white-washed graves, who outwardly indeed appear beautiful, and inside are full of bones of the dead and all uncleanness.
28 So you also outwardly indeed are manifested righteous to men, and inside you are full of hypocrisy and lawlessness.
29 Woe to you, scribes and Pharisees, hypocrites, because you build the graves of the prophets, and adorn the grave monuments of the righteous,
30 And say, If we had been in the days of our fathers, we absolutely would not have been partakers with them in the blood of the prophets.
31 Therefore you are witnesses to yourselves, that you are the children of those murdering the prophets,
32 And you fill up the measure of your fathers.
33 Snakes! Offspring of vipers, how shall you escape from the judgment of hell?
34 Therefore, behold, I set apart and send to you prophets, and wise ones, and scribes, and some of them you will kill and crucify, and some of them you will scourge in your synagogues and pursue from city to city,
35 That upon you may come all the righteous blood poured upon the earth, from the blood of righteous Abel to the blood of Zacharias, son of Barachias, whom you murdered between the temple and the altar.
36 Amen, I say to you, All these things will come upon this generation.
37 Jerusalem, Jerusalem, the one killing the prophets, and stoning the ones set apart and sent to her, how often I willed to gather your children together, in the manner a hen gathers her brood

under the wings, and you absolutely willed not to!
38 Behold, your house is left to you a wasteland,
39 Because I say to you, You will absolutely not see me from now on until you will say, Blessed is the one coming in the name of the Lord."

We can see is just one of the several sermons Jesus preached against them. The gravamen of Jesus' charge against the Pharisees was that they did, in fact, scrupulously follow the ritual laws of Judaism, but their scrupulousness did not make them more charitable or lead to inner repentance.

Jesus sought to call his followers to a more inward form of obedience, in which righteous acts stemmed from an inward love of God, rather than a desire to please others, to seem holy in their eyes, or for a fear of temporal or divine retribution.

Thus we are to follow the Law of God and in doing so we are then living in righteousness. Some preach the law instead of the gospel. Some modify them and preach neither the law nor the gospel. Some think the law is the gospel, and some think the gospel is the law; those who hold these views are not clear on either.

There are many questions in which one may ask in understanding the importance of the Law and the Gospel.

Has not the law been fully abrogated by the coming of Christ into the world?

Would you bring us under that heavy yoke of bondage which none has ever been able to bear?

Does not the New Testament expressly declare that we are not under the law but under grace?

That Christ was made under the law to free His people there from?

Is not an attempt to over-awe men's conscience by the authority of the law a legalistic imposition, altogether at variance with that Christian liberty which the Saviour has brought in by His obedience unto death?

The answer is in Matthew 5:17-18; *"Do not suppose that I came to loosen down the law or the prophets; I absolutely did not come to loosen down, but to fulfil. Because, Amen, I say to you, Until heaven and earth pass away, one iota or one particle will absolutely not pass away from the law until all comes to be."*

We can see that the Christian is not under the law as a covenant of works nor as a ministration of condemnation, but he is under it as a rule of life and an objective standard of righteousness for all people for all times. This makes it important.

What does sanctified behaviour consist of?

It consists in pleasing God.

What is it that pleases God?

The doing of His will.

Where is His will to be discerned?

It will be discerned in His Holy Law.

The law, then, is the Christian's rule of life, and the believer finds that he delights in the law of God after the inward man.

Rom. 7:22; *"Because I delight in the law of God according to the inward man,"*

The Christian is not lawless but *"under the law to Christ",*

1 Cor. 9:21; *"To those without law, as without law, not being without law to God, but in the law of Christ, that I might gain those without law."*

Sin is lawlessness, and salvation is the bringing of the lawless one into his true relation to God, within the blessedness of His holy law. The Law of Moses is not other than the law of Christ; it is an objective standard just as Christ is our pattern.

The Ten Commandments were honoured by God, founded in love, and are obeyed out of affection for the One who provided redemption. The reason for this is that there is a need for a fixed, objective, moral standard.

The moral law carries permanent validity since it is an objective standard uniquely sanctioned by God and goes straight to the root of our moral problems. It lays its finger on the church's deepest need in evangelism as well as in the Christian life: sanctification.

The Ten Commandments are desperately needed not only in the church but also in society. We live in a lawless age and lawlessness reigns in the home, in the church, in the school, and in the land.

The Scriptures tell us that *"righteousness exalts a nation, but sin is a reproach to any people."*

The Ten Commandments are the only true standard of righteousness.

What is meant by Moral measure?

Tragically, there are some Christians who have contributed to our society's moral decline by removing the Ten Commandments from their instruction. The law restrains sin. Without the moral law this world would be a field of blood, as is evidenced in place where there is no regard for God's commands.

Where do we find the will of God in respect to morality?

We will find the will of God in respect to morality only in the Ten Commandments.

This subject, law and gospel, is in the highest degree, important and edifying, both to saints and to sinners. To know it experimentally, is to "be wise unto salvation;" and to live habitually under the influence of it, is to be at once holy and happy.

To have spiritual and distinct views of it, is the way to be kept from verging toward self-righteousness, on the one hand, and licentiousness, on the other; and to be enabled to assert, the absolute freeness of sovereign grace, and at the same time, the sacred interests of true holiness. Without an experimental knowledge, and an unfeigned faith, of the law and the gospel, a man can neither venerate the authority of the one, nor esteem the grace of the other.

The law and the gospel are the principal parts of Divine Revelation; or rather, they are the centre, the sum, and the substance, of the whole. Every passage of sacred Scripture is either law or gospel; or is capable of being referred, either to the one or to the other.

Even the Histories of the Old and New Testaments, so far as the creation of man, are deemed ast narratives of facts, done in conformity, or in opposition, to the moral law, and done in the belief, or disbelief, of the gospel.

The ordinances of the ceremonial law, given to the ancient Israelites, were, for the most part, grafted on the Second and Fourth Commandments of the moral law; and in their typical reference, were an obscure revelation of the gospel.

The precepts of the judicial law, are all reducible to commandments of the moral law, and especially, to those of the second table. All threatenings, whether in the Old or in the New Testament, are threatenings either of the law, or of the gospel; and in every promise, is a promise either of the one, or of the other.

Every prophecy of Scripture is a declaration of things obscure, or future, connected either with the law or the gospel, or with both. And there is not, in the sacred Volume, one admonition, or reproof, or exhortation, but what refers, either to the law or the gospel, or to both.

If then, a man cannot distinguish aright, between the law and the gospel; he cannot rightly understand, so much as a single article of Divine truth.

If he does not have spiritual and just apprehensions of the holy law, he cannot have spiritual and transforming discoveries of the glorious gospel; and, on the other hand, if his views of the gospel be erroneous or wrong, his notions of the law cannot be right.

Besides, if the speculative knowledge, of the law and the gospel, be superficial and indistinct, they will often be in danger of mingling the one with the other and they will, in a greater degree than can be conceived, retard their progress in holiness, as well as in peace and comfort.

But on the contrary, if they can distinguish well, between the law and the gospel, they will thereby, under the illuminating influences of the Holy Spirit, be able, to discern the glory of the whole scheme of redemption; to reconcile all passages of Scripture which appear contrary to each other; to try doctrines whether they are of God; to calm their own consciences in seasons of mental trouble; and to advance resolutely in evangelical holiness and spiritual consolation.

It is important to consider the difference between the law and the gospel as well as the agreement between them. The establishment of the law by the gospel, or the subservience of the gospel to the authority and honour of the law must be addressed.

The believer's privilege of being dead to the law as a covenant of works, with a necessary consequence of it is very important.

To emphasize this importance of the law in terms of the Ten Commandments below are statements of testimony regarding three witnesses.

1. Testimony of David

David, a man after God's own heart--the sweet singer of Israel.

Ps. 119:35; "*Make me to go in thy path of thy commandments; for therein do I delight*"

Ps. 119:53; "*Indignation has taken hold of me Because of the wicked, who forsake Your law.*"

Ps. 119:97; "*Oh, how I love Your law! It is my meditation all the day*"

Ps. 119:113; "*I hate the double-minded, But I love Your law*"

Ps. 119:126; "*It is time for You to act, O LORD, For they have regarded Your law as void*"

2. Testimony of Paul

Our Lord's chief apostle—Paul.

Rom. 3:31; "*Do we then make void the law through faith? Certainly not! On the contrary, we establish the law*"

Rom. 7:12; "*Therefore the law is holy and the commandment holy and just and good*"

Rom. 7:22; "*For I delight in the law of God according to the inward man*"

Gal. 3:24; "*Therefore the law was our tutor to bring us to Christ, that we might be justified by faith*"

3. Testimony of Jesus

Our Lord Himself

Mt. 5:17-18; "*Do not think that I came to destroy the Law or the Prophets. I did not come to destroy but to fulfil. For assuredly, I say to you, till heaven and earth pass away, one jot or one title will by no means pass from the law till all is fulfilled*"

We often hear the expression, "Be like Jesus."

What was He like?

He was perfect.

How do we know?

We must have a perfect standard by which to judge and that perfect standard is the perfect law of God

Ps. 19:7; "*The law of Jehovah is complete, converting the soul; the testimony of Jehovah is faithful, making the open wise.*"

The Testimony of the importance of the law and the Gospel is in the bible itself. In that the whole Bible is either law or gospel, or law and gospel related.

The history of the Old and New Testaments, as far as man is concerned, is nothing more than narratives of lives lived in conformity or opposition to the moral law, or lived in belief or unbelief of the gospel. All the threatenings of the Old and New Testaments are threatenings either of the law or of the gospel.

John 3:18; *"He who believes in Him is not condemned; but he who does not believe is condemned already, because he has not believed in the name of the only begotten Son of God"*

2 Thess. 1:7-9; *"...when the Lord Jesus is revealed from heaven with His mighty angels, in flaming fire taking vengeance on those who do not know God, and on those who do not obey the gospel of our Lord Jesus Christ. These shall be punished with everlasting destruction from the presence of the Lord and from the glory of His power"*

Every prophecy of Scripture is a declaration of things obscure and future and is connected with either law or gospel. Every promise is a promise related to either the law or the gospel, or both. Every good admonition, reproof, or exhortation is with reference to the law or the gospel, or both.

Thus the law and the gospel are the centre, the sum, and the substance of the whole Bible.

How important then is it properly to relate and distinguish the two?

The closer we get to a clear view of the difference between the law and the gospel, and the connection between them as they serve to establish each other, the more we will understand the Holy Scriptures and thus the will and mind of God, and the more useful we will be in His service.

Another indication of the importance of the law is that it reveals the two kinds of knowledge that are necessary for salvation:

1. The law reveals the character of God. God's law comes from His nature. The nature of God determines what is right, and the will of God imposes that standard upon all His creatures as a moral obligation. Since his will flows from His nature, and the law is perfect.

Ps. 19:7; *"The law of Jehovah is complete, converting the soul; the testimony of Jehovah is faithful, making the open wise."*

The law reflects the perfection of his nature.

Man is not answerable to an abstract law, but to God. Behind the law is the Lawgiver.

Therefore, to find fault with the law is to find fault with the Lawgiver. The law is not the arbitrary edicts of a capricious despot, but the wise, holy loving precepts of one who is jealous for His glory and for the good of His people.

Christ was perfect.

How do we know?

He kept the law perfectly--He was the law personified. Christ perfectly manifests the Father :

Col. 2:9; *"For in Him dwells all the fullness of the Godhead bodily"*

2. The law reveals the condition of man. To walk up to someone and say, *"All have sinned"* does

not bring conviction unless that person knows what sin is.

1 John 3:4; *"Sin is the transgression of the law"*

Rom. 3:20; *"By the law is the knowledge of sin"*

The knowledge of sin as violation of God's law brings conviction. The whole Bible is law and gospel, and the two are so vitally related to each other that an accurate knowledge of either cannot be obtained without the other.

The law reveals the character of God and the condition of man. These two kinds of knowledge are absolutely necessary for salvation. The law is essential to true biblical evangelism because by the law is the knowledge of sin. It was the law that was effective in Paul's conversion:

Rom. 7:7; *"I would not have known sin except through the law"*

The law is the only biblical rule and direction for obedience that is, a sanctified life.

What does sanctified behaviour consist of?

Doing the will of God

What is the will of God in respect to morality?

The moral law summarized in the Ten Commandments.

The law is one of three truths of the Bible that stand or fall together:

1. The law of God,
2. The cross of Christ,
3. The righteous judgment of almighty God.

First, if there is no law there is no sin because sin is the transgression of the law that is The Ten Commandments.

Second, if there is no cross there is no hope for poor sinners in other words no forgiveness of sin.

Third, if there is no righteous judgment of almighty God who cares about sin or a Saviour. These three truths stand or fall together.

Law and Grace

Romans 5:20; *"Moreover the law entered, that the offence might abound. But where sin abounded, grace did much more abound."*

There is no point upon which men make greater mistakes than upon the relation which exists between the law and the gospel. Some men put the law instead of the gospel: others put the gospel instead of the law; some modify the law and the gospel, and preach neither law nor gospel: and others entirely abrogate the law, by bringing in the gospel.

Many there are who think that the law is the gospel, and who teach that men by good works of benevolence, honesty, righteousness, and sobriety, may be saved. On the other hand, many teach that the gospel is a law; that it has certain commands in it, by obedience to which, men are meritoriously saved; such men err from the truth, and understand it not.

A certain class maintains that the law and the gospel are mixed, and that partly by observance of the law, and partly by God's grace, men are saved. These men understand not the truth, and are false teachers.

The two questions we need to understand and consider are:

1. What is the design of the law?
2. What is the end of the gospel?

The coming of the law is explained in regard to its objects: *"Moreover the law entered, that the offence might abound."*

Then comes the mission of the gospel: *"But where sin abounded, grace did much more abound."*

To understand this fully we need to consider the fact that it effects the world at large and the entrance of the law into it; and then afterwards, effecting the heart of the convinced sinner, and the entrance of the law into the conscience.

What is meant by concerning the world?

The object of God in sending the law into the world was *"that the offence might abound."* But then comes the gospel, for *"where sin abounded, grace did much more abound."*

In reference to the entire world, God sent the law into the world *"that the offence might abound."*

There was sin in the world long before God sent the law. God gave his law that the offence might seem to be an offence; ay, and that the offence might abound exceedingly more than it could have done without its coming. There was sin long before Sinai smoked; long before the mountain trembled beneath the weight of Deity, and the dread trumpet sounded exceeding loud and long, there had been transgression.

And where that law has never been heard, in heathen countries where that word has never gone forth, there is sin, because, though men cannot sin against the law which they have never seen, they can all rebel against the light of nature, against the dictates of conscience, and against that traditional remembrance of right and wrong, which has followed mankind from the place where

God created them.

All men, in every land, have consciences, and therefore all men can sin. The ignorant Hottentots, who has never heard anything of a God, has just so much of the light of nature, that in the things that are outwardly good or bad he will discern the difference; and though he foolishly bows down to stocks and stones, he has a judgment which, if he used it, would teach him better.

If he chose to use his talents, he might know there is a God; for the Apostle, when speaking of men who have only the light of nature, plainly declares in Romans 1:20 that *"the invisible things of him, from the creation of the world, are clearly seen, being understood by the things that are made, even his eternal power and Godhead; so that they are without excuse."*

Without a divine revelation men can sin, and sin exceedingly conscience, nature, tradition, and reason, being each of them, sufficient to condemn them for their violated commandments.

The law makes no one a sinner; all men are such in Adam, and were so practically before its introduction. It entered that *"the offence might abound."* Upon hearing this statement seems a very terrible thought at first sight, and many Christians would have shirked this text altogether.

But when we read the bible and we read verses that we do not understand, we should think of it as a text and study it; and then try to seek it out before the heavenly Father, and then when he has opened it to the soul, It is a duty to communicate it to us, with the holy aid of the Spirit. *"The law entered that the offence might abound."*

How does the law makes offenses "abound."?

First of all, the law tells us that many things are sins which we should never have thought to be so if it had not been for the additional light. Even with the light of nature, and the light of conscience, and the light of tradition, there are some things we should never have believed to be sins had we not been taught so by the law.

According to Spurgeon; *"Now, what man by light of conscience, would keep holy the Sabbath-day—suppose he never read the Bible, and never heard of it? If he lived in a South Sea island he might know there was a God, but not by any possibility could he find out that the seventh part of his time should be set apart to that God.*

We find that there are certain festivals and feasts among heathens and that they set apart days in honour of their fancied gods; but I should like to know where they could discover that there was a certain seventh day to be set apart to God, to spend the time in his house of prayer.

How could they, unless indeed, tradition may have handed down the fact of the original consecration of that day by the creating Jehovah. I cannot conceive it possible that either conscience or reason could have taught them such a command as this: Remember the Sabbath-day to keep it holy.

Six days shalt thou labour, and do all thy work; but the seventh day is the Sabbath of the Lord thy God, in it thou shalt not do any work, thou, nor thy son, nor they daughter, thy manservant, nor they maidservant, nor thy cattle, nor thy stranger that is within thy gates.

Moreover, if in the term "law" we comprehend the ceremonial ritual, we can plainly see that many things, in appearance quite indifferent, were by it constituted sins. The eating of animals that do not chew the cud and divide the hoof, the wearing of linsey-woolsey, the sitting on a bed polluted by a leper—with a thousand other things, all seem to have no sin in them, but the law made them into sins, and so made the offence to abound."

Secondly it is a fact which we can verify by looking at the workings of our own mind, that law has a tendency to make men rebel. Human nature rises against restraint.

If we had not known lust except the law had said, *"Thou shalt not covet."* The depravity of man is excited to rebellion by the promulgation of laws.

We are so evil, that we conceive at once the desire to commit an act, simply because it is forbidden. Children, we all know, as a rule, will always desire what they may not have, and if forbidden to touch anything, will either do so when an opportunity serves, or will long to be able to do so. The same tendency is applied to any human nature which can discern in to man-kind at large.

Is then the law chargeable with our sins?

The answer is in Romans 7:7, 8, 11 which states *"But sin, taking occasion by the commandment, wrought in me all manner of concupiscence. For sin taking occasion by the commandment deceived me, and by it slew me."*

The law is holy, and just, and good, it is not faulty, but sin uses it as an occasion of offence, and rebels when it ought to obey.

During the reign of Augustine he placed the truth in a clear light when he wrote *"The law is not in fault, but our evil and wicked nature; even as a heap of lime is still and quiet until water be poured thereon, but then it begins to smoke and burn, not from the fault of the water, but from the nature and kind of the lime which will not endure it."*

Therefore we need to see this as a sense in which the entrance of the law causes the offence to abound.

Thirdly the law increases the sinfulness of sin, by removing all excuse of ignorance.

Until men know the law, their crimes have at least a palliation of partial ignorance, but when the code of rules is spread before them, their offenses become greater, since they are committed against light and knowledge. He who sins against conscience shall be condemned; of how much sorer punishment shall he be thought worthy who despises the voice of Jehovah, defies his sacred sovereignty, and wilfully tramples on his commands.

The more light the greater guilt. The law affords that light, and so causes us to become double offenders. Oh, the nations of the earth who have heard the law of Jehovah, our sin is increased, and our offence abounds.

Some say, *"How unwise it must have been that a law should come to make these things abound!"*

Does it not, at first sight, seem very harsh that the great author of the world should give us a law which will not justify, but indirectly cause our condemnation to be greater?

Does it not seem to be a thing which a gracious God would not reveal, but would have withheld?

But, we need to know and understand *"that the foolishness of God is wiser than men;"* and understand that there is a gracious purpose even here. Naturally men dream that by a strict performance of duty they shall obtain favour, but God said: *"I will show them their folly by proclaiming a law so high that they will despair of attaining unto it. They think that works will be sufficient to save them. They think falsely, and they will be ruined by their mistake. I will send them a law so terrible in its censures, so unflinching it its demands, that they cannot possibly obey it, and they will be driven even to desperation, and come and accept my mercy through Jesus Christ.*

They cannot be saved by the law not by the law of nature. As it is, they have sinned against it. But yet, I know, they have foolishly hoped to keep my law, and think by works of the law they may be justified; whereas I have said, 'By the works of the law no flesh living can be justified;' therefore I will write a law—it shall be a black and heavy one—a burden which they cannot carry; and then they will turn away and say, 'I will not attempt to perform it; I will ask my Saviour to bear it for me.'"

We need to imagine that some young men are about to go to sea, where they will meet with a storm. Suppose you and I was put into a position where we may cause a tempest before the other shall arise. Well, by the time the natural storm comes on, those young men will be a long way out at sea, and they will be wrecked and ruined before they can put back and be safe.

Yet when they are just at the mouth of the river, we send a storm, putting them in the greatest danger, and precipitating them ashore, so that they are saved.

Thus did God.

He sends a law which shows them the roughness of the journey. The tempest of law compels them to put back to the harbour of free grace, and saves them from a most terrible destruction, which would otherwise overwhelm them.

The law never came to save men. It never was its intention at all. It came on purpose to make the evidence complete that salvation by works is impossible, and thus to drive the elect of God to rely wholly on the finished salvation of the gospel.

Now, to illustrate this, we all remember those high mountains called the Alps. Well, it would be a great mercy if those Alps were a little higher. It would have been, at all events, for Napoleon's soldiers when he led his large army over, and caused thousands to perish in crossing.

Now, if it could have been possible to pile another Alps on their summit, and make them higher than the Himalaya, would not the increased difficulty have deterred him from his enterprise, and so have adverted the destruction of thousands.

Napoleon demanded, *"Is it possible?" "Barely possible,"* was the reply.

"Avancez," cried Buonaparte; and the host were soon toiling up the mountain side.

Now, by the light of nature, it does seem possible for us to go over this mountain of works, but all men would have perished in the attempt, the path even of this lower hill being too narrow for mortal footsteps. God, therefore, puts another law, like a mountain, on the top; and now the sinner says, *"I cannot climb over that. It is a task beyond Herculean might. I see before me a narrow pass, called the pass of Jesus Christ's mercy the pass of the cross I think I will follow that."*

But if it had not been that the mountain was too high for him, he would have gone climbing up, and climbing up, until he sank into some chasm, or was lost under some mighty avalanche, or in some other way perished eternally.

But the law comes that the whole world might see the impossibility of being saved by works.

What is meant by Grace?

Firstly, Grace excels sin in the numbers it brings beneath its sway. It is my firm belief that the number of the saved will be far greater than the damned. It is written that in all things Jesus shall have pre-eminence; and **why is this left out?**

Can we think that Satan will have more followers than Jesus?

Oh, no; for while it is written that the redeemed are a number that no man can number; it is not recorded that the lost are beyond numeration. It is true however that, we know that the visible elect are ever a remnant but then there are others to be added.

Think for a moment of the army of infant souls who are now in heaven. These all fell in Adam, but being all elect, were all redeemed and regenerated, and were privileged to fly from the mother's breasts to glory. Happy, are we who are spared might well envy.

Nor let it be forgotten that the multitudes of converts in the millennial age will very much turn the scale.

For then the world will be exceedingly populous, and a thousand years of a reign of grace might easily suffice to overcome the majority accumulated by sin during six thousand years of its tyranny. In that peaceful period, when all shall know him, from the least even unto the greatest, the sons of God shall fly as doves to their windows, and the Redeemer's family shall be exceedingly multiplied.

What of those who have been deluded by superstition, and destroyed by lust, must be counted by thousands, but grace has still the pre-eminence.

Saul has slain people in his thousands, but David in his ten-thousands. We admit that the number of the damned will be immense, but we do think that the two states of infancy and millennial glory will furnish so great a reserve of saints that Christ shall win the day.

The procession of the lost may be long; there must be thousands, and thousands, and thousands, of those who have perished, but the greater procession of the King of kings shall be composed of larger hosts than even these.

"Where sin abounded, grace did much more abound."

The trophies of free grace will be far more than the trophies of sin. Yet Grace does "much more abound," because a time shall come when the world shall be all full of grace; whereas there has never been a period in this world's history when it was wholly given to sin.

When Adam and Eve rebelled against God, there was still a display of grace in the world; for in the garden at the close of the day, God said, *"I will put enmity between thee and the woman, and between thy seed and her seed; it shalt bruise thy head, and thou shall bruise his heel;"* and since that first transgression, there has never been a moment when grace has entirely lost its footing in the earth.

God has always had his servants on earth; at times they have been hidden by fifties in the caves, but they have never been utterly cut off. Grace might be low; the stream might be very shallow, but it has never been wholly dry.

There has always been a salt of grace in the world to counteract the power of sin. The clouds have never been so universal as to hide the day. But the time is fast approaching when grace shall extend all over our poor world and be universal.

According to the Bible testimony, we look for the great day when the dark cloud which has swathed this world in darkness shall be removed, and it shall shine once more like its entire sister planets. It has been for many a long year clouded and veiled by sin and corruption; but the last fire shall consume its rags and sackcloth. After that fire, the world in righteousness shall shine.

The huge molten mass now slumbering in the bowels of our common mother shall furnish the means of purity. Palaces, and crowns, and peoples, and empires, are all to be melted down; and after like a plague-house, the present creation has been burned up entirely, God will breathe upon the heated mass, and it will cool down again.

He will smile on it as he did when he first created it, and the rivers will run down the new-made hills, the oceans will float in new-made channels; and the world will be again the abode of the righteous for ever and for ever.

This fallen world will be restored to its orbit; that gem which was lost from the sceptre of God shall be set again, yea, he shall wear it as a signet about his arm. Christ died for the world; and what he died for, he will have.

He died for the whole world, and the whole world he will have, when he has purified it and cleansed it and fitted it for himself. *"Where sin abounded, grace did much more abound;"* for grace shall be universal, whereas sin never was.

Has the world lost its possessions by sin?

It has gained far more by grace. Even though we have been expelled from the Garden of Eden; a place where peace, love, and happiness found a glorious habitation; We need to remember that the Garden of Eden is not ours, with its luscious fruits, its blissful bowers, and its rivers flowing o'er sands of gold, but we have through Jesus a fairer habitation.

He has made us sit together in heavenly places the plains of heaven exceed the fields of paradise in the ever-new delights which they afford, while the tree of life and the river from the throne render the inhabitants of the celestial regions more than imparadised.

Did we lose natural life and subject ourselves to painful death by sin?

Has not grace revealed an immortality for the sake of which we are too glad to die?

Life lost in Adam is more restored in Christ. We admit that our original robes were rent in sunder by Adam, but Jesus has clothed us with a divine righteousness, far exceeding in value even the spotless robes of created innocence.

We mourn our low and miserable condition, through sin, but we will rejoice at the thought, that we are now more secure than before we fell, and are brought into closer alliance with Jesus than our standing could have procured us.

O Jesus! Who has won us an inheritance more wide than our sin has ever lavished. Your grace has overtopped our sins. *"Grace doth much more abound."*

What is meant by the entrance of the law into the heart?

We have to deal carefully when we come to deal with internal things; it is not easy to talk about this little thing, the heart. When we begin to meddle with the law of their soul, many become indignant, but we do not fear their wrath.

We are going to attack the hidden man. The law entered their hearts that sin might abound, *"but where sin abounded, grace did much more abound."*

The law causes the offence to abound by discovering sin to the soul. When once God the Holy Ghost applies the law to the conscience, secret sins are dragged to light, little sins are magnified to their true size, and things apparently harmless become exceedingly sinful.

Before that dread searcher of the hearts and Trier of the reins makes his entrance into the soul, it appears righteous, just, lovely, and holy; but when he reveals the hidden evils, the scene is changed. Offenses which were once styled peccadilloes, trifles, freaks of youth, follies, indulgences, little slip, then appear in their true colour, as breaches of the law of God, deserving condign punishment.

John Bunyan says in his famous allegory the Pilgrims Progress:

"Then the Interpreter took Christian by the hand and led him into a very large parlour that was full of dust, because never swept; in which after he had reviewed it a little while, the Interpreter called for a man to sweep.

Now, when he began to sweep, the dust became so abundantly to fly about, that Christian had almost therewith been choked.

Then said Interpreter to a damsel that stood by, 'Bring hither water, and sprinkle the room'; the which when she had done, it was swept and cleansed with pleasure.

Then said Christian, 'What means this?'

The Interpreter answered, 'This parlour is the heart of a man that was never sanctified by the sweet grace of the gospel.

The dust is his original sin and inward corruptions that have defiled the whole man. He that began to sweep, at first, is the law; but she that brought the water and did sprinkle it,
is the gospel. Now, whereas thou sawest that as soon as the first began to sweep, the dust did so fly about, that the room could not by him be cleansed, but that thou wast almost choked therewith; this is to show thee, that the law, instead of cleansing the heart (by its working) from sin, doth revive,

Romans 7:9, *"And I was alive separate from law at one time, and when the commandment came sin revived, and I died."*

Put strength into,

1 Corinthians 15:56, *"And the sting of death is sin, and the power of sin is the law."*
And increase it in the soul,

Romans 5:20, *"And law came in alongside that the transgression might abound. But where sin abounded, grace super-abounded,"*

Even as it doth discover and forbid it, for that doth not give power to subdue. Again, as thou sawest the damsel sprinkle the room with water, upon which it was cleansed with pleasure; this is to show thee, that when the gospel comes in the sweet and precious influences thereof to the heart, then, I say, even as thou sawest the damsel lay the dust by sprinkling the floor with water, so is sin vanquished and subdued, and the soul made clean, through the faith of it, and consequently fit for the King of glory to inhabit.'"

The heart is like a dark cellar, full of lizards, cockroaches, beetles, and all kinds of reptiles and insects, which in the dark we see not, but the law takes down the shutters and lets in the light, and so we see the evil.

Thus sin becoming apparent by the law, it is written the law makes the offence to abound. We need to understand that the law, when it comes into the heart, shows us how very black we are. Some of us know that we are sinners. It is very easy to say it.

The word "sinner" hath only two syllables in it, and there are many who frequently have it on their lips, but who do not understand it. They see their sin, but it does not appear exceedingly sinful till the law comes. We think there is something sinful in it; but when the law comes, we detect its abomination.

The questions we need to consider and answer honestly are:

Has God's holy light ever shone into your souls?

Have you had the fountains of your great depravity and evil broken up, and been wakened up sufficiently to say, "O God! I have sinned?"

Now, if there are those whom have had their hearts broken up by the law, we will find the heart is more deceitful than the devil.

The Bible says, *"The heart is deceitful above all things."* The devil is one of the things; therefore, it is worse than the devil *"and desperately wicked."*

How many of us do we find saying, *"Well, I trust I have a very good heart at the bottom. There may be a little amiss at the top, but I am very goodhearted at bottom."*

If we saw some fruit on the top of a basket that was not quite good, would you buy the basket because they told us, *"Yes, but they are good at the bottom*?"

"No, no," we would say, *"they are sure to be best at the top, and if they are bad there, they are sure to be rotten below."*

There are many people who live queer lives, and some friends say, *"He is good-hearted at the bottom; he would get drunk sometimes, but he is very good-hearted at the bottom."*

Ah! Never believe it.

Men are often estimated better than they seem to be. If the outside of the cup or platter is clean, the inside may be dirty, but if the outside is impure, you may always be sure the inside is no better.

Most of us put our goods in the window or keep all our good things in the front, and bad things behind. We need to stop making excuses about ourselves, about the badness of our hearts, if the law has entered into our soul, bow down and say, *"O the sin— O the uncleanness—the blackness—the awful nature of our crimes!" "The law entered that the offence may abound."*

The law reveals the exceeding abundance of sin, by discovering to us the depravity of our nature. We are all prepared to charge the serpent with our guilt, or to insinuate that we go astray, from the force of ill for example.

But the Holy Spirit dissipates these dreams by bringing the law into the heart. Then the fountains of the great deep are broken up, the chambers of the imagery are opened, the innate evil of the very essence of fallen man is discovered.

The law cuts into the core of the evil, it reveals the seat of the malady, and informs us that the leprosy lies deep within. Oh! How the man abhors himself when he sees all his rivers of water turned into blood, and loathsomeness creeping over all his being.

He learns that sin is no flesh wound, but a stab in the heart; he discovers that the poison has impregnated his veins, lies in his very marrow, and hath its fountain in his inmost heart. Now he loathes himself, and would fain be healed.

Actual sin seems not half so terrible as in-bred sin, and at the thought of what he is, he turns pale, and gives up salvation by works as impossibility.

Thus having removed the mask and shown the desperate case of the sinner, the relentless law causes the offence to abound yet more by bringing home the sentence of condemnation. It mounts the judgment seat, puts on the black cap, and pronounces the sentence of death. With a harsh unpitying voice it solemnly thunders forth the words, *"Condemned already."*

It bids the soul prepare its defence, knowing well that all apologies have been taken away by its former work of conviction. The sinner is therefore speechless, and the law, with frowning looks, lifts up the veil of hell, and gives the man a glimpse of torment. The soul feels that the sentence is just, that the punishment is not too severe, and that mercy it has no right to expect; it stands quivering, trembling, fainting, and intoxicated with dismay, until it falls prostrate in utter despair.

The sinner puts the rope around his own neck, arrays himself in the attire of the condemned, and throws himself at the foot of the King's throne, with but one thought, *"I am vile"*; and with one prayer, *"God be merciful to me a sinner."*

We can see that the law does not cease its operations even here, for it renders the offence yet more apparent by discovering the powerlessness occasioned by sin. It not only condemns but it actually kills.

He who once thought that he could repent and believe at pleasure, finds in himself no power to do either the one or the other. When Moses smites the sinner he bruises and mangles him with the first blow, but at a second or a third, he falls down as one dead.

Moreover, when we are in the grave which the law has digged for us, we feel as if we did not feel, and we grieve because we cannot grieve.

The dread mountain lies upon us which renders it impossible to stir hand or foot, and when we would cry for help our voice refuses to obey us. In vain the minister cries, *"Repent,"* Our hard heart will not melt; in vain he exhorts us to believe; that faith of which he speaks seems to be as much beyond our capacity as the creation of the universe.

Ruin is now become ruin indeed. The thundering sentence is in our ears, *"CONDEMNED ALREADY,"* another cry follows it, *"DEAD IN TRESPASSES AND SINS,"* and a third, more awful and terrible, mingles its horrible warning, *"The wrath to come—the wrath to come."*

The sinner he is now cast out as a corrupt carcass, he expects each moment to be tormented by the worm that never dies and to lift up his eyes in hell.

Now is mercy's moment, and we turn the subject from condemning law to abounding grace.

Listen, O heavy laden, condemned sinner, while in my Master's name, I publish super abounding grace. Grace excels sin in its measure and efficacy. Though your sins are many, mercy has many pardons. Though they excel the stars, the sands, the drops of dew in their number, one act of remission can cancel all.

Your iniquity, though a mountain, shall be cast into the midst of the sea. Your blackness shall be washed out by the cleansing flood of your Redeemer's gore.

Mark! I said YOUR sins, and I meant to say so, for if you are now a law condemned sinner, I know you to be a vessel of mercy by that very sign. Oh, hellish sinners, abandoned profligates, off-casts of society, outcasts from the company of sinners themselves, if you will only acknowledge your iniquity, here is mercy, broad, ample, free, immense, INFINITE.

Remember this O sinner,
"If all the sins that men have done,
In will, in word, in thoughts, in deed,
Since words were made, or time began,
Were laid on one poor sinner's head.
The stream of Jesus' precious blood
Applied, removes the dreadful load."

Yet again, grace excelled sin in another thing. Sin shows us its parent, and tells us our heart is the father of it, but grace surpasses sin there, and shows the Author of grace the King of kings.

The law traces sin up to our heart; grace traces its own origin to God, and his love and grace.

What a blessing grace is?

For its source is in the everlasting mountains. Sinner, if you are the vilest in the world, if God forgives you this morning, you will be able to trace your pedigree to him, for you will become one of the sons of God, and have him always for your Father.

God himself sees you as a wretched criminal at the bar, and I hear mercy cry, "Discharge him!" He is pallid, halt, sick, maimed, heal him. He is of a vile race, I will adopt him into my family.

Sinner! God takes you for his son. What, of it that you are poor, God says, "I will take you to be mine for ever. You shall be my heir. This is you brother. In ties of blood he is one with Jesus and he is our actual brother!"

Yet how come this has change?

Oh! Is that not an act of mercy?

"Grace did much more abound."
"Grace has put me in the number Of the Saviour's family."
Grace outdoes sin, for it lifts us higher than the place from which we fell.
And again, "where sin abounded, grace did much more abound"; because the sentence of the law may be reversed, but that of grace never can.

I stand here and feel condemned, yet, perhaps, I have a hope that I may be acquitted. There is a dying hope of acquittal still left. But when we are justified, there is no fear of condemnation.

I cannot be condemned if I am once justified; fully absolved I am by grace. I defy Satan to lay hands on me, if I am a justified man. The state of justification is an invariable one, and is indissolubly united to glory.

Who shall lay anything to the charge of God's elect?

It is God that justified.

Who is he that condemned?

It is Christ that died, rather, than he is risen again, who is even at the right hand of God who also makes intercession for us.

Who shall separate us from the love of Christ?

Shall tribulation, or distress, or persecution, or famine, or nakedness, or sword?

In all these things we are more than conquerors through him that loves us. For I am persuaded that neither death, nor life, nor angels, nor principalities, nor powers, nor things present, nor things to come, nor height, nor depth, nor any other creature, shall be able to separate us from the love of God, which is in Christ Jesus our Lord.

Oh! Poor condemned sinner, does this not charm, and make you fall in love with free grace?

And all this is YOURS.

Your crimes, if once blotted out, shall never be laid to your charge again. The justification of the gospel is no Armenian sham, which may be reversed if you should in future turn aside.

No; the debt once paid, cannot be demanded twice—the punishment, once endured, cannot again be inflicted. Saved, saved, saved, entirely saved by divine grace, you may walk without fear the wide world over.

Furthermore, just as sin makes us sick, and grievous, and sad, so does grace make us far more joyful and free? Sin causes one to go about with an aching heart, till he seems as if the world would swallow him, and mountains hang above ready to drop upon him.

This is the effect of the law. The law makes us sad; the law makes us miserable.

But, poor sinner, grace removes the evil effects of sin upon your spirit, if only we believe in the Lord Jesus Christ, and we shall go out of this place with a sparkling eye and a light heart.

I remember well the morning when I stepped into a little place of worship, as miserable almost as hell could make me being ruined and lost. I had often been at chapels where they spoke of the law, but I heard not the gospel. I sat down the pew a chained and imprisoned sinner; the Word of God came, and I went out free. Though I went in miserable as hell, I went out elated and joyful. I sat there black; I went away whiter than driven snow. God had said, *"Though your sins are as scarlet, they shall be whiter than snow."*

Why not this is my lot, brothers and sisters, if you feel yourself as a sinner now?

It is all he asks of thee, to feel the need of him, this he has, and now the blood of Jesus lies before us all.

"The law has entered that sin might abound."

You are forgiven, only believe it; elect, only believe it; 'it is the truth that you are saved.

And now, lastly, poor sinner, has sin made you unfit for heaven?

Grace shall render thee a fit companion for seraphs and the just made perfect. You, who are today lost and destroyed by sin, shall one day find yourself with a crown upon your head and a golden harp in your hand, exalted to the throne of the Most High. Think, if only you will repent, there is a crown laid up for you in heaven.

If you are feeling guilty, lost and depraved, are condemned in your conscience by the law?

Then I invite you, in my Master's name, to accept pardon through his blood.
He suffered in your stead, he has atoned for your guilt and you are acquitted.
You are an object of his eternal affection; the law is but a schoolmaster, to bring us all to Christ. Bring yourself to him.
Fall into the arms of saving grace. No works are required, no fitness, no righteousness, no doings. You are complete in him who said, "It is finished."

In the words of Spungeon;

"Ye debtors whom he gives to know
That you ten thousand talents owe,
When humble at his feet you fall,
Your gracious God forgives them all.
"Slaves that have borne the heavy chain
Of sin, and hell's tyrannical reign,
To liberty assert your claim,

And urge the great Redeemer's name."
"The rich inheritance of heaven,
Your joy, your boast, is freely given;
Fair Salem your arrival waits,
With golden streets and pearly gates."
"Her blest inhabitants no more
Bondage and poverty deplore!

No debt, but love immensely great;
Their joy still rises with the debt."
Amen

Understanding the Law and the Gospel

Matthew 5:19 says; *"Whoever therefore will make one of these least commandments loose, and teaches men in this way, he shall be called the least in the kingdom of heaven, and whoever does and teaches them, this one will be called great in the kingdom of heaven."*

The words make…loose, luoo in Greek, to loose, is meaning to make loose so as to remove it. Jesus in these words says that ministers of His Word who teach that the Law of God as given to Moses is not important will be called least in the kingdom of heaven, and those who teach the Law of God as given to Moses will be called great in the kingdom of heaven.

In the experiences of many there are far too many of God's ministers who have taken a non-biblical view of Paul's teachings, and taught either directly or by their neglect that God's Law as given to Moses is not applicable today.

Many preach only the "New" Testament, and consider the "Old" Testament as not important. They neither study it, nor preach it. The reason is that they do not understand what Jesus did. Jesus states very clearly that He did not come to loosen down the law, but to fulfill it,

Matthew 5:17, *"Do not suppose that I came to loosen down the law or the prophets; I absolutely did not come to loosen down, but to fulfill."*

Jesus further declares that not one iota or one particle will pass away until all comes to be; not only in the life of Jesus, but also in the life of the believer, as well as ultimately in the new heaven and the new earth.

We cannot be saved by keeping the Law, because no one has ever lived perfect on this earth except Jesus. That is why Jesus came, to do what we could not do - to do that for us.

Upon taking Him, His Holy Spirit creates within us a new spirit and nature, and enables us to obey His law. Only the most deceived antinomian would argue that we are exempt from obeying the Ten Commandments since we have become Christians.

We are not now as a new born believer free to commit adultery, steal, and violate all the rest of God's commandments, because Jesus fulfilled the Law for us, Rom 6:1; *"What therefore shall we speak? Shall we stay in sin that grace may super-abound?"*

We need to understand that there is one Law, God's Law. There never have been two, nor will there ever be. The same Law of God given to Israel is the same Law given to all, and applicable to all,

Numbers 15:16; *"One law and one judgment shall be for you and for the stranger who lodges with you."*

The law of Jehovah is complete, converting the soul,

Psalm 19:7; *"The law of Jehovah is complete, converting the soul; the testimony of Jehovah is faithful, making the open wise."*

The Law of Moses only claimed completeness or perfection in the coming of the Messiah to pour out His blood in the perfect sacrifice to fulfil every detail prophesied in the Law of Moses.

The error the Pharisees and others espoused in Jesus' day was that they thought that their outward efforts to outwardly conform to God's Law would save them, rejecting the Holy Spirit conviction that they had not been able to perfectly keep God's Law even outwardly much less in their hearts, and rejecting God's Messiah who was the fulfilment of every Law of sacrificial blood ever pictured in any animal sacrifice, as well as perfectly fulfilling the moral law, and all the rest of the law.

There is only one Law, but for purposes of understanding the Law it can be divided into the moral Law, the ceremonial Law, the civil Law, and the health Law. We are more responsible for the moral Law today than ever before because of its complete fulfilment and revelation in the life of Jesus, and our receiving a holy nature enabling us to live it out in our lives.

The ceremonial Law was fulfilled to the last detail in the Lord Jesus, and we reap its blessings in the present Priestly ministry of the Lord Jesus, and His shed blood now effective in the Holy of Holies in heaven, where we are to boldly enter constantly to receive grace,

Hebrews 10:19; *"Having therefore, brothers, outspokenness for entrance into the sanctuary in the blood of Jesus,"*

The civil Law which God gave to govern Israel, to protect the innocent, to punish the guilty, and to control the spread of lawlessness and chaos, is perfect, and far superior to the laws of any modern government.

The health Law given by God to maintain health by eating habits, and washings to cleanse away disease and maintain health, and obedience to, and faith in, all of God's moral, civil, and spiritual laws to receive and maintain healing, is far superior to any medical science anywhere in the modern world.

So we must not quote Saint Paul that we are not under law, but under grace,

Romans 6:14; *"Because sin will absolutely not lord it over you, because you are absolutely not under the law, but under grace."*

In order to support the lax attitudes that we have adopted towards God's Law, we need to study it in order to fully understand it. It is very clear that God allowed His Temple in Jerusalem to literally be demolished,

Matthew 24:2; *"And Jesus said to them, Do you absolutely not see all these things? Amen, I say to you, Absolutely not a stone upon a stone will be left here, which will absolutely not be loosened down."* (AD 70), and prevented the Jews from building it again to pressure them to see the true Temple in the Lord Jesus Who made the once for all sacrifice,

Hebrews 10:10; *"In which will we are sanctified through the offering of the body of Jesus Christ on one single occasion."* and who now ministers for them and us as the Priest before the face of God in heaven,

Hebrews 4:14; *"Therefore having a great head priest, having gone through the heavens, Jesus, the Son of God, let us hold our confession,"*

The Law of God will never pass away,

Matthew 5:17-18, *"Do not suppose that I came to loosen down the law or the prophets; I absolutely did not come to loosen down, but to fulfill. Because, Amen, I say to you, Until heaven and earth pass away, one iota or one particle will absolutely not pass away from the law until all comes to be."*

And includes every word spoken by Jesus and the Apostles to explain it,

Matthew 7:12; *"Therefore all things whatever you will that men should do to you, even so you also do to them, because this is the law and the prophets."*

Its heart is love,

Matthew 22:37-40; *"And Jesus said to him, You shall love the Lord your God in all your heart, and in all your soul, and in all the exercise of your mind.*
38 This is the first and great commandment.
39 And the second is like it, You shall love your neighbour as yourself.
40 In these two commandments hang all the law and the prophets."

It was never contradicted by Jesus or the Apostles, but they contradicted only the Pharisees' wrong understanding of the Law,

Acts 6:13; *"And they stood false witnesses, saying, This man absolutely does not stop speaking words of blasphemy against this holy place and the law,"*

Acts 18:13; *"Saying that, He incites men to worship God contrary to the law."*

The law prophesied as also the prophets prophesied,

Matthew 11:13; *"Because all the prophets and the law prophesied until John."*

Devout men in the apostolic age obeyed the Law,

Acts 22:12; *"And a certain Ananias, a devout man according to the law, having a good testimony of all the Jews dwelling there,"*

Acts 24:14; *"But this I confess to you, that according to the way which they call a party, so I officially minister to the God of my fathers, believing all things according to the written law and prophets;"*

Acts 25:8; *"Defending himself, he said, Absolutely not against the law of the Jews, and absolutely not against the temple, and absolutely not against Caesar, have I sinned anything."*

The Apostles preached only out of the Law and the Prophets, because they wrote the Gospels, the Acts, the Epistles, and the Revelation; God's Law was not only given to Moses and Israel upon tablets of stone, but also written in the hearts of all men upon the face of the earth,

Romans 2:15; *"Who show the work of the law written in their hearts, their conscience witnessing with them, and their calculations between one another formally charging them or else defending them,"*

No flesh can be justified by the law, but all men come to the knowledge of sin by the Law,

Romans 3:20; *"On this very account, out of the deeds of the law there will absolutely no flesh be justified before his face, because through the law is full knowledge of sin."*

Romans 5:20; *"And law came in alongside that the transgression might abound. But where sin abounded, grace super-abounded,"*

Paul is horrified at the suggestion that he would make void the Law,

Romans 3:31; *"Therefore do we render the law inoperative through faith? We do not! On the contrary, we cause the law to stand."*

So he establishes it; we are not free from the Law, but free from sin and guilt of violating the Law,

Romans 6:18-23; *"And being made free from sin, you were made servants of righteousness.*
19 I speak as a man because of the weakness of your flesh, because as you stand your members alongside as servants to uncleanness and of lawlessness into lawlessness, even so now stand your members alongside as servants of righteousness into holiness,
20 Because when you were the servants of sin, you were free from righteousness.
21 Therefore what fruit did you have then in those things of which you are now ashamed? Because the end of those things is death.
22 And now being set free from sin and made servants to God, you have your fruit into holiness, and the end everlasting life,
23 Because the wages of sin is death, and the gift of God is eternal life in Christ Jesus our Lord."

Romans 7:3-4; *"So therefore if, the husband living, she is to another man, according to divine oracle she is an adulteress, and if the husband dies she is free from that law, so that, being to another man, she is not an adulteress. Therefore, my brothers, you also were made dead to the law through the body of Christ, into becoming married to another, to the one raised out of the dead, that we may bear fruit to God,"*

Romans 8:2; *"Because the law of the Spirit of life in Christ Jesus has set me free from the law of sin and death,"*

The fleshly mind is not subject to the Law,

Romans 8:7; *"On this very account the fleshly mind is hostile against God, because it absolutely will not arrange itself under the law of God, because it absolutely does not have the power."*

But the mind renewed by the Holy Spirit fulfils the Law,

Romans 8:4; *"That the righteous deeds of the law might be fulfilled in us, who walk not according to the flesh, but according to the Spirit,"*

Romans 13:8-10; *"Do not owe anyone anything, except to love one another, because the one loving another has fulfilled the law,*
9 Because this, Absolutely do not commit adultery, Absolutely do not murder, Absolutely do not steal, Absolutely do not bear false witness, Absolutely do not covet, and if any other commandment, it is summed up in this word, You shall love your neighbour as yourself.
10 Love absolutely does not work any evil to his neighbour; love therefore is the fulfilment of the law."

No man can be saved by our works of the Law,

Galatians 2:16-21; *"Having seen that a man is absolutely not justified out of law works, but through*

Jesus Christ's faith, we also have believed into Jesus Christ, so that we may be justified out of Christ's faith, and absolutely not out of law works, because out of law works absolutely no flesh will be justified.
17 And if, seeking to be justified in Christ, we ourselves also were found sinners, is then Christ the minister of sin? It shall not be.
18 Because if I build up again the things which I loosened down, I cause myself to stand as a violator,
19 Because I through the law am dead to the law, that I may live to God.
20 I am crucified with Christ, and I live; absolutely no longer I, but Christ lives in me, and the life I now live in the flesh, I live in the faith of the Son of God, the one loving me, and giving himself over for me.
21 I absolutely do not set aside the grace of God, because if righteousness is through the law, then Christ is dead for nothing."

Galatians 3:10-12; *"Because as many as are out of law works are under a curse, because it has been written, Cursed is everyone who absolutely does not continue in all things which are written in the scroll of the law to do them.*
11 And that absolutely no one is justified in the law alongside of God, it is clear, because, The righteous will live out of faith.
12 And the law is absolutely not out of faith, but, The man doing them shall live in them."

And Christ has redeemed us from the curse of the Law,

Galatians 3:14-15; *"That the blessing of Abraham might be to the races in Christ Jesus, that we might take the promise of the Spirit through faith.*
15 Brothers, I speak according to man, Even a man's covenant made authoritative, absolutely no one sets aside, or adds to it."

The Law is not against the promises of God,

Galatians 3:21; *"Is the law therefore against the promises of God? It shall not be, because if there had been a law given which had power to make alive, truly righteousness would have been out of the law."*

The Law is the servant bringing us to Christ,

Galatians 3:24; *"Thus the law was our guardian into Christ, that we might be justified out of faith."*

Anyone trying to save himself by the Law falls short of reaching grace,

Galatians 5:14; *"Because all the law is fulfilled in the one word: You shall love your neighbour as yourself."*

The Law is beautifully good, if you use it lawfully,

1 Timothy 1:8; *"And we see that the law is beautifully good, if anyone uses it lawfully;"*

What Saint Paul was fighting against was a wrong use of the Law by people in their attempt to save themselves by good works rather than trusting Jesus the fulfilment of the Law.

The only parts of the Law not completely stated again in the New Covenant as binding upon all believers are the dietary laws, the laws of animal sacrifice [which are fulfilled in Christ], and the

Sabbath laws. Dietary and Sabbath laws are left to the individual judgment of the believer as to whether or not he will keep those,

Colossians 2:16; *"Therefore do not let anyone judge you in food, or in drink, or in sharing of a festival, or a new moon festival, or of the Sabbaths,"*

All of these are festivals from the Law of Moses. This verse in no way gives believers permission to attend idolatrous festivals. Paul's instructions are that believers (Hebrews or ethnics) could participate or not participate in Mosaic festivals, and were not to be judged by other believers who did or by believers who did not.

The Sabbath is the only Commandment of the Ten that is not restated in the New Covenant as binding upon Christian believers. I believe that God will bless any believer who observes the Sabbath for the right heart reasons, but no one must make Sabbath (Saturday) or Sunday observance a condition of salvation or even of complete obedience to God.

We are not to forsake the assembling of ourselves together for public worship of God, and the preaching of the good news of His Son,

Hebrews 10:25; *"Not forsaking the assembling of ourselves together, as the habit of some, but comforting, and so much the more, as you see the day drawing near,"*

Many ministers prefer the traditional assembling of the church on Sunday, but there is nothing in the New Covenant that says a believer who goes to church services on Sunday is more obedient than a believer who attends church services on another day or night.

The Sabbath was definitely not included by the Apostles in their instructions in Acts 15, and here is the only place that deals with in any of the apostolic writings in the bible.

What are the Laws of the Kingdom?

A kingdom like any nation today cannot function without laws. There must be a standard of conduct for subjects and citizens to follow, or chaos and anarchy would result.

Following the laws of a kingdom or nation does not grant a person citizenship that is not the purpose of law. Law is simply a guide for people to follow to ensure cohesion, agreement, and peace in civil and interpersonal relationships.

Without an understood standard, enforced by a sovereign ruler, everyone would act according to his own whim or desire, and nothing good or worthwhile would be produced.

Judges 21:25; *"In those days there was no king in Israel; every man did right in his eyes."*

The Kingdom of God is no different. God is not the author of confusion

I Corinthians 14:33; *"Because God is not the God of tumults, but the God of peace, as in all churches of the saints."*

His Kingdom will be peaceful and orderly because everyone who will enter into it will have voluntarily submitted himself to the law the commandments of God. God will not have anyone in His Kingdom who demonstrates, by the pattern of his life, that he will not obey Him

Matthew 7:21-23; *"Not everyone saying to me, Lord, Lord, will enter into the kingdom of heaven, but those doing the will of my Father who is in heaven.*
22 Many will speak to me in that day, Lord, Lord, did we absolutely not prophesy in your name, and in your name throw out demons, and in your name did many works of power?
23 And then I will confess to them that, I absolutely never knew you; depart from me, those working lawlessness."

Hebrews 10:26-31; *"Because if we are sinning voluntarily after taking the knowledge of the truth, there is left absolutely no more sacrifice for sins,*
27 But a certain fearful expectation for judgment and fiery zeal, which is about to eat those opposed.
28 Anyone setting aside the law of Moses died apart from pity upon two or three witnesses;
29 Of how much more revenge, do you think, will he be entitled, who has trampled under the Son of God, and has governed the blood of the covenant, in which he was sanctified, common, and has insulted the Spirit of grace?
30 Because we see the one who said, Vengeance is mine; I will give back, says the Lord. And again, The Lord will judge his people. 31 It is a fearful thing to fall into the hands of the living God."

Revelation 12:17; *"Saying, We give you thanks, Lord God, the Almighty, the one who is, and the one who was, and the one who is coming, because you took your great power, and reigned."*

We can see in this passage that it describes the saints as those "who keep the commandments of God and have the testimony of Jesus Christ."

A Pharisee once asked Jesus, "Teacher, which is the great commandment in the law?"

Matthew 22:36; *"Teacher, which is the great commandment in the law?"*

His response shows that the intent behind God's law is love, love towards God, and love toward fellow man:

Jesus said to him, *"'You shall love the LORD your God with all your heart, with all your soul, and with your entire mind.' This is the first and great commandment. And the second is like it: 'You shall love your neighbour as yourself.' On these two commandments hang all the Law and the prophets."* Matthew 22:37-40

These two statements loving God and loving neighbour as oneself encapsulate the first four and the last six commandments respectively. The commandments merely define further how to love God and love man.

We love God in general by placing Him first, by not adopting physical aids in worshipping Him, by not bearing His name in vain, and by keeping the seventh-day Sabbath holy. We love man, in general, by honouring our parents, not murdering, not committing adultery, not stealing, not lying, and not coveting.

When Jesus Christ came, He revealed the spirit the intent of His law. He showed that the sixth commandment extends much further than merely prohibiting the taking of human life, but covers even hating

Matthew 5:21-22; *"You heard that it has been spoken to the ancients, Absolutely do not murder, and whoever murders shall be liable in the judgment; And I say to you, That everyone who is provoked to anger with his brother without cause shall be liable in the judgment, and whoever says to his brother, You are bad, shall be liable to the Sanhedrin, and whoever says, Fool, shall be liable to hell fire."*

Similarly, the intent behind the seventh commandment is to stop adultery at its source: the heart

Matthew 5:27-28; *"You heard that it was spoken to the ancients, Absolutely do not commit adultery; And I say to you, That everyone looking at a woman to set his passion upon her has committed adultery with her already in his heart."*

Following God's commandments in both their letter and spirit ensures the best quality of life for everyone. When Jesus was asked what one must do to have eternal life, His response was simple: *"If you want to enter into [eternal] life, keep the commandments"* Matthew 19:17.

To reinforce this, in His last words to the disciples before His arrest and crucifixion, He had much to say about keeping God's commandments. He was giving them (and us) instruction that would not be absolved by His death:

"If you love Me, keep My commandments." John 14:15

"He who has My commandments and keeps them, it is he who loves Me. And he who loves Me will be loved by My Father, and I will love him and manifest Myself to him." John 14: 21

"If anyone loves Me, he will keep My word; and My Father will love him, and We will come to him and make Our home with him. He who does not love Me does not keep My words; and the word which you hear is not Mine but the Father's who sent Me." John 14:23-24

The apostle James calls the Ten Commandments "the royal law" which means that it came from a King, and is worthy of His Kingdom: If we really fulfil the royal law according to the Scripture, we shall obey all the commandments that God had given to Moses on Mt Sinai.

While a man cannot earn entrance into God's Kingdom that is a gift that God must bestow

Ephesians 2:8; *"Because by grace you are saved, through faith, and that absolutely not out of yourselves; it is the gift of God,"*

It is plain from these Scriptures that wilful rebellion against God's standard of righteousness will keep a man out of the Kingdom:

"Now the works of the flesh are evident, which are: adultery, fornication, uncleanness, licentiousness, idolatry, sorcery, hatred, contentions, jealousies, outbursts of wrath, selfish ambitions, dissensions, heresies, envy, murders, drunkenness, revelries, and the like; of which I tell you. .. that those who practice such things will not inherit the kingdom of God." Galatians 5:19-21

I Corinthians 6:9-10 includes *"homosexuals (catamites), sodomites, thieves, coveters, and extortionists in the list of those who will be barred from entering the Kingdom of God."*

Revelation 21:8 mentions that *"the cowardly, the unbelieving, and the abominable will not live eternally."*

Revelation 22:15 adds *"whoever loves and practices a lie."*

These examples show that there is a standard of conduct by which God expects the heirs to His

Kingdom to live. After all, eternal life is more than just length of days living forever would be a terrible curse if there were not also quality of life to match it.

Our Saviour tells us what He means by eternal life: *"And this is eternal life that they may know you, the only true God, and Jesus Christ whom You have sent"* John 17:3.

In Amos 5:4, God exclaims, *"Seek Me and live!"* He is saying, *"Turn to Me and My way of life; seek to know Me,"* not *"Search for Me."* He is saying, *"Seek to know Me by living the same way I do."* That is how experiential knowledge of Him becomes an intimate knowing of Him. We know Him, in large part, by living the same law of love that He lives by

The law and Jesus

Matthew 5:17-19; "*Do not suppose that I came to loosen down the law or the prophets; I absolutely did not come to loosen down, but to fulfil.*
18 Because, Amen, I say to you, Until heaven and earth pass away, one iota or one particle will absolutely not pass away from the law until all comes to be.
19 Whoever therefore will make one of these least commandments loose, and teaches men in this way, he shall be called the least in the kingdom of heaven, and whoever does and teaches them, this one will be called great in the kingdom of heaven."

The questions in which we need to think about are:

What is the status of Mosaic Law since the coming of Jesus Christ?

In what ways did He affect it, if at all?

How did the revelation which Jesus brought relate to that of Moses?

We can see that the answer to these questions lies in Matthew 5:17-19; "*Do not suppose that I came to loosen down the law or the prophets; I absolutely did not come to loosen down, but to fulfil.*
18 Because, Amen, I say to you, Until heaven and earth pass away, one iota or one particle will absolutely not pass away from the law until all comes to be.
19 Whoever therefore will make one of these least commandments loose, and teaches men in this way, he shall be called the least in the kingdom of heaven, and whoever does and teaches them, this one will be called great in the kingdom of heaven."

It is important that we memorise this passage this is central to the law and the gospel in which has been addressed earlier.

However in this passage Jesus specifically disclaims any conflict between Himself and Moses and enthusiastically affirms His harmonious relationship with the older revelation.

One prominent feature of in the Gospel of Matthew is the close association of Jesus with Moses and the Torah. In terms of narrative and teaching. We can see that when Jesus as an infant had a narrow escape.

Mathew.2: 19-21; *"And Herod having expired, behold, a heavenly messenger of the Lord is manifested by a dream to Joseph in Egypt,*
20 Saying, Rising up, take to your side the child and his mother, and go into the land of Israel, because those seeking the soul of the infant have died.
21 And he, rising up, took the infant and his mother to his side, and came into the land of Israel."

In comparison with Moses in Exodus 2: 5-11; *"And the daughter of Pharaoh came down to bathe at the river, and her maids walked by the hand of the river; and she saw the box among the papyrus reeds, and she sent her maid to take it.*
6 And she opened it, and she saw the male child; and behold, the baby wept; and she spared him out of pity, and said, This is one of the male children of the Hebrews.
7 And his sister said to Pharaoh's daughter, Shall I walk, and call a nurse for you of the Hebrew women, that she may nurse the boy baby for you?
8 And Pharaoh's daughter said to her, Walk. And the maid walked, and called the boy baby's mother.

9 And Pharaoh's daughter said to her, Walk away with this child, and nurse him for me, and I will give you your wages; and the woman took the boy baby, and nursed him.
10 And the boy baby became large, and she brought him to Pharaoh's daughter, and he was her son; and she called his name Moses, for she said, Because I pulled him out of the water.
11 And it was in those days, that Moses was grown, and he went out to his brothers, and saw their burdens; and he saw an Egyptian man striking a Hebrew man of his brothers."

We can see that from the two scriptures that there is a slight reminiscent of that of Moses and that of Jesus. All baby boys were ordered to be killed. Yet God saved Moses and Jesus.

There are many other references in the bible that show Jesus had come to fulfil the law. Jesus' responses to Satan in the wilderness temptation are all from "Israel in the wilderness passages"

Matthew 4:4, *"And he judging for himself said, It has been written, Man shall absolutely not live by bread alone, but on every spoken word that goes out through the mouth of God."*

Matthew 4:7, *"Jesus said to him, Again it has been written, You shall absolutely not tempt the Lord your God."*

Matthew 4:10; *"Then Jesus says to him, Go away, Satan, because it has been written, You shall prostrate yourself to the Lord your God, and to him only you will officially minister."*

Deuteronomy.8:3; *"And he looked down upon you with harshness, and allowed you to hunger, and fed you with manna, which you did not know by seeing, neither did your fathers know by seeing, so that he might make you know by seeing that man does not live by food alone, but man lives by every word that goes out of the mouth of Jehovah."*

Deuteronomy.6:16; *"You shall not put Jehovah, your God, to the test, as you tested him in Massah."*

Deuteronomy.10:20; *"You shall fear Jehovah, your God; you shall serve him, and you shall cling to him, and you shall swear by his name.*"

The time that Jesus spent in the wilderness follows the baptism in water and the fast for forty days and precedes the giving of the law.

This in comparison with Moses proceeds in the same direction: childhood, exodus through the Red Sea/baptism in the Jordan, wilderness temptation, mountain, law. The temptations also are common to both: hunger and idolatry. Both Moses and Jesus fasted forty days on the mountain.

Matthew 4:2; *"And having fasted forty days and forty nights, afterward he hungered."*

Exodus 24:18; *"And Moses went into the midst of the cloud, and went up into the mount; and Moses was in the mount forty days, and forty nights."*

Deuteronomy 9:9; *"When I went up into the mountain to receive the tablets of stone, the tablets of the covenant which Jehovah cut with you, and I dwelt in the mountain forty days and forty nights, I did not eat food, and I did not drink water;"*

And as an ethical teacher Jesus resembles Moses more in Matthew than in any of the other Gospels. The Moses/Sinai motif is extensive and quite beyond coincidence. Matthew labours to present Jesus Christ in close association with Moses.

However, Moses is by no means the only historical point of reference found in the Gospel of Matthew.

There is also Abraham

Matthew 1:1; *"The scroll of the generation of Jesus Christ, the son of David, the son of Abraham."*

David

Matthew1:1; *"The scroll of the generation of Jesus Christ, the son of David, the son of Abraham."*

Matthew 12:3-4; *"And he said to them, Did you absolutely not read what David did when he himself hungered and the ones with him, How he entered into the house of God and ate the loaves set forth, which was absolutely not lawful for him to eat, neither for the ones with him, except for the priests only?"*

The priests and the temple

Matthew 12:5-6, *"Or did you absolutely not read in the law that on the Sabbaths the priests in the temple profane the Sabbath and are innocent? And I say to you, That one greater than the temple is in this place."*

Jonah

Matthew 12:39-41, *"And he answering said to them, An evil and adulterous generation seeks a sign, and absolutely no sign will be given to it, except the sign of the prophet Jonah,*
40 Because just as Jonah was in the belly of the huge fish three days and three nights, so the Son of Man will be in the heart of the earth three days and three nights.
41 Men of Nineveh will stand in the judgment with this generation and will condemn it because they repented at the preaching of Jonah, and behold, one greater than Jonah is here."

Solomon

Matthew 12:42, *"The queen of the south will be raised up in the judgment with this generation and will condemn it, because she came out from the extremities of the earth to hear the wisdom of Solomon, and behold, a greater than Solomon is here."*

And Elijah

Matthew 17:1-12; *"And after six days Jesus took to himself Peter, James, and John, his brother, and takes them up into a high mountain privately,*
2 And was transformed in front of them, and his face shined as the sun, and his garments became white as the light.
3 And behold, they were gazing at Moses and Elijah talking with him.
4 And Peter answering, said to Jesus, Lord, it is beautifully good for us to be here; if you will, let us make here three tents, one for you, and one for Moses, and one for Elijah.
5 While he was speaking, behold, a cloud full of light overshadowed them, and behold a voice out of the cloud, saying, This is my beloved Son, in whom I am well pleased; hear him.
6 And the disciples hearing it fell upon their face and feared exceedingly.
7 And coming near, Jesus touched them, and said, Rise up, and do not fear.
8 And lifting up their eyes, they saw absolutely no one except Jesus alone.

9 And they coming down from the mountain, Jesus commanded them, saying, Tell no one the vision until the Son of Man is raised out from the dead.
10 And his disciples asked him, saying, Why then do the scribes say that Elijah must come first?
11 And Jesus answering, said to them, Elijah indeed comes first, and will restore all things.
12 And I say to you, That Elijah even now has come, and they absolutely did not recognize him, but did in him whatever they willed. Thus also the Son of Man is about to suffer many things under them."

What is striking in all of these is not just the typological reference but the nature of the type's realization.

It is amazing to see how when we look at Jesus and the law how the bible begins to fit together both the Old covenant and the New Covenant. Jesus, for example, is not merely another great Solomon: he is "greater than Solomon"

Matthew 12:42; *"The queen of the south will be raised up in the judgment with this generation and will condemn it, because she came out from the extremities of the earth to hear the wisdom of Solomon, and behold, a greater than Solomon is here."*

Likewise, He is "greater than the temple"

Matthew 12:6, *"And I say to you, That one greater than the temple is in this place."*

And "greater than Jonah"

Matthew 12:41; *"Men of Nineveh will stand in the judgment with this generation and will condemn it because they repented at the preaching of Jonah, and behold, one greater than Jonah is here."*

We can also see that He is also David's greater Son

Matthew 12:3-4; *"And he said to them, Did you absolutely not read what David did when he himself hungered and the ones with him, How he entered into the house of God and ate the loaves set forth, which was absolutely not lawful for him to eat, neither for the ones with him, except for the priests only?"*

In fact, this is precisely what Jesus' points out in Matthew 22:45 where he states; *"If therefore David calls him Lord, how is he his son?"*

Furthermore, He is "Lord even of the Sabbath"

Matthew 12:8; *"Because the Son of Man is Lord of the Sabbath."*

We can see that from the bible Jesus is not only a son of Abraham He is the Son of Abraham par excellence, the One in Whom the Patriarchal promises reach their goal

Matthew 1:1; *"The scroll of the generation of Jesus Christ, the son of David, the son of Abraham."*

He is not simply a representative of Israel He is the true Israel

Matthew 2:15-18; *"And he was there until the end of Herod, that the spoken word by the Lord through the prophet might be fulfilled, saying, Out of Egypt I have called my son.*
16 Then Herod seeing that he was mocked by the sacred astronomers, was exceedingly enraged,

and setting apart and sending, he took away all the male children, those in Bethlehem, and in all its borders, from two years and downwards, according to the time which he had ascertained with the sacred astronomers.
17 Then the spoken word by Jeremiah, the prophet, was fulfilled, saying,
18 A voice was heard in Rama, lamenting, and weeping, and much moaning, Rachel sobbing aloud for her children, and absolutely not willing to be comforted, because they absolutely were not."

His name is "Joshua," but He is greater than his forebear and brings a greater deliverance: "for He shall save His people from their sins"

Matthew 1:21; "*And she will give birth to a son, and you shall call his name Jesus, because he will save his people from their sins."*

Moreover, it would have been very wrong to erect booths for each of Moses, Elijah and Jesus: these men, great as they were, deserve no equal place with the Christ.

Matthew 17:5; *"While he was speaking, behold, a cloud full of light overshadowed them, and behold a voice out of the cloud, saying, This is my beloved Son, in whom I am well pleased; hear him."*

He is greater than Elijah and greater than Moses; that is to say, greater than the prophets and even the law itself.

Matthew makes it clear in his Gospel the important emphasis on Jesus' personal authority. This is involved the references to David, Solomon, Moses, Joshua, etc., mentioned above. Whatever authority these men had, Jesus' is greater.

But there is more. With the clear reference to the commandments given to Moses at Mt Sinai we can see in Jesus, God Himself speaking from the mountain.

In Jesus' opening statement "I came to fulfil" and repeated "But I say unto you" is an unmistakable claim of authority. This is precisely the effect it had on the original hearers.

Matthew7:28-29; *"And it was, when Jesus had finished with these words, the crowd was struck with shock over his teaching,*
29 Because he was teaching them as one having authority, and not as the scribes."

We can see from this passage that Only God the Father, the Son, and the Holy Spirit have absolute authority. Jesus as the Son of Man and as the Son of God on earth never acted with absolute authority.

He always did what He did by delegated authority, authority delegated to Him by God the Father as an obedient man. Of course, His power was derived from the Holy Spirit and the Father according to the divine arrangement, arranged by God from all eternity for Him to fulfil our obligations to God's righteous law and nature.

Jesus constantly confessed that He did absolutely nothing on His own, but only as He saw the Father do, and as He heard the Father say, in John 8:28 – 29; *"Therefore Jesus said to them, When you have lifted up the Son of Man, then you will know that I AM, and from myself I do absolutely not one thing, but just as my Father taught me, I say these things. And the one sending me is with me; the Father absolutely did not leave me alone, because I always do the things pleasing him."*

We do not have absolute authority. We have no authority to do anything unless the authority to do it has been specifically delegated to us by God and His Word, John 3:27; *"John answered and said, A man absolutely does not have the power to take anything unless it is given to him out of heaven."*

However, in concluding the Sermon "these sayings of mine" which constitute the standard by which men are judged as we can see recorded in Matthew 7:24-27, *"Therefore everyone who hears these words of mine, and does them, I will cause him to become like a cautiously thoughtful man, who built his house upon a massive rock;*
25 And the rain came down, and the streams came, and the winds blew hard, and fell against that house; and it absolutely did not fall, because it had been founded upon a massive rock.
26 And everyone hearing these words of mine, and does not do them will become like a stupid man who built his house upon the sand,
27 And the rain came down, and the streams came, and the winds blew hard, and struck against that house, and it fell, and its crash was great." and it is disobedience to His word which constitutes "lawlessness"

Matthew 7:23; *"And then I will confess to them that, I absolutely never knew you; depart from me, those working lawlessness."*

We can see clearly that Jesus is stressing His personal right to articulate what is the law of God and how it must be kept. His great authority is precisely the point in 12:8: *"The Son of man is lord even of the Sabbath."* That is, He has authority over the law itself, with inherent right to do with it as He sees fit.

In fact, the entire issue over the Sabbath in chapter 12 shows that His authority surpasses even that of the law. This point is emphasized again on the Mount of Transfiguration.

Matthew 17:1-12; *"And after six days Jesus took to himself Peter, James, and John, his brother, and takes them up into a high mountain privately,*
2 And was transformed in front of them, and his face shined as the sun, and his garments became white as the light.
3 And behold, they were gazing at Moses and Elijah talking with him.
4 And Peter answering, said to Jesus, Lord, it is beautifully good for us to be here; if you will, let us make here three tents, one for you, and one for Moses, and one for Elijah.
5 While he was speaking, behold, a cloud full of light overshadowed them, and behold a voice out of the cloud, saying, This is my beloved Son, in whom I am well pleased; hear him.
6 And the disciples hearing it fell upon their face and feared exceedingly.
7 And coming near, Jesus touched them, and said, Rise up, and do not fear.
8 And lifting up their eyes, they saw absolutely no one except Jesus alone.
9 And they coming down from the mountain, Jesus commanded them, saying, Tell no one the vision until the Son of Man is raised out from the dead.
10 And his disciples asked him, saying, Why then do the scribes say that Elijah must come first?
11 And Jesus answering, said to them, Elijah indeed comes first, and will restore all things.
12 And I say to you, That Elijah even now has come, and they absolutely did not recognize him, but did in him whatever they willed. Thus also the Son of Man is about to suffer many things under them."

We can see in Exodus 24:16; *"And the heavy glory of Jehovah lodged upon Mount Sinai, and the cloud covered it six days; and he called to Moses the seventh day out of the midst of the cloud."*

That there is a similarity between Jesus and Moses again with regards to the six days, the mountain, the Divine presence and voice, the cloud, the shining face, the divine revelation.

But the climactic event is the voice from Heaven demanding that this Jesus, by virtue of His very Person, must be heard and obeyed: "*This is my beloved Son, in whom I am well pleased; hear Him.*" This phrase is to stress again the fact of Jesus' authority.

Therefore in His missionary manifesto of Matthew 28:18-20; *"And coming near, Jesus talked with them, saying, All authority was given to me in heaven and upon earth.*
19 Having gone therefore, disciple all the races, baptizing them into the name of the Father, and of the Son, and of the Holy Spirit,
20 Teaching them to keep all things whatever I have commanded you, and behold, I am with you all the days, to the entire completion of the age. Amen."

We can see that Jesus lays claim to universal authority 28:18; *"And coming near, Jesus talked with them, saying, All authority was given to me in heaven and upon earth."*

And in this global discipline enterprise it is all of His commandments which are to be taught and kept.

Matthew 28:20; "*Teaching them to keep all things whatever I have commanded you, and behold, I am with you all the days, to the entire completion of the age. Amen."*

We can see in Deuteronomy 18:18-22; *"I will raise up a Prophet for them from the midst of their brothers, like you, and will give my words in his mouth, and he shall speak to them all that I command him.*
19 And it shall be, what man will not attentively hear my words which he shall speak in my name, I will tread searching him out.
20 But the prophet which shall boil over to speak a word in my name which I have not commanded him to speak, or that shall speak in the name of other gods, even that prophet shall die.
21 And if you say in your heart, How shall we know by seeing the word which Jehovah has not spoken?
22 When a prophet speaks in the name of Jehovah, if the word does not become and does not come, that is the word which Jehovah has not spoken; the prophet has spoken it arrogantly; you shall not fear him"

There Moses Himself prophesied of One like him but greater Who would come and, like him, give the law of God. It was this One Whose law would be brought to bear in judgment. His authority is supreme, and His law is obligatory.

We can see in looking at the Gospel of Matthew how he presents Jesus as the new Moses and as a new Law-giver. But He is much greater than Moses and even Moses' law. He bears a supreme authority that is His by inherent right. And it is within this Context that Jesus is presented as the "fulfiller" of the law.

What are the most important factors in understanding the meaning of what Jesus said in Matthew 5:17-20?

One of the most important factors in making a determination of the meaning of Jesus' sermon in 5:17-20 is the very passage that follows:

Matthew 5:21-48; *"You heard that it has been spoken to the ancients, Absolutely do not murder, and whoever murders shall be liable in the judgment;*
22 And I say to you, That everyone who is provoked to anger with his brother without cause shall be liable in the judgment, and whoever says to his brother, You are bad, shall be liable to the

Sanhedrin, and whoever says, Fool, shall be liable to hell fire.
23 If therefore you offer your gift upon the altar, and there remember that your brother has anything against you,
24 Leave there your gift in front of the altar, and go away; first be reconciled to your brother, and then coming, offer your gift.
25 In haste be in a good mind with your opponent while you are with him in the way, lest at any time the opponent gives you over to the judge, and the judge to the subordinate officer, and you be thrown into prison.
26 Amen, I say to you, You will absolutely not at all come out of there until you pay the last kodrantes.
27 You heard that it was spoken to the ancients; Absolutely do not commit adultery;
28 And I say to you, That everyone looking at a woman to set his passion upon her has committed adultery with her already in his heart.
29 And if your right eye offends you, tear it out, and throw it from you, because it is advantageous for you that one of your members should be destroyed, and not your whole body be thrown into hell.
30 And if your right hand offends you, chop it off, and throw it from you, because it is advantageous for you that one of your members should be destroyed, and not your whole body be thrown into hell.
31 And it was spoken, Whoever sets free his wife, let him give her a divorce;
32 And I say to you, That whoever sets free his wife without the word of sexual promiscuity makes her commit adultery, and whoever shall marry the one set free commits adultery.
33 Again, you have heard that it has been spoken to the ancients, Absolutely do not commit perjury, but give over your oaths to the Lord;
34 And I say to you, Do not swear at all, not even by the heaven, because it is his throne;
35 Not even by the earth, because it is the footstool of his feet; not even by Jerusalem, because it is the city of the great King.
36 Do not even swear by your head, because you absolutely do not have power to make one hair white or black.
37 And let your word be, Yes, yes; no, no, and whatever is more than these is out of the evil one.
38 You heard that it was spoken, An eye for an eye, and a tooth for a tooth;
39 And I say to you, Do not stand against the evil, but whoever slaps you on your right cheek, turn around to him also the other.
40 And the one deciding to sue you and take away your tunic, let him also take your cloak.
41 And whoever will compel you into public service one mile, go on with him two.
42 Give to the one asking you, and from the one deciding to borrow from you, do not turn away.
43 You heard that it was spoken, You shall love your neighbour, and shall hate the one who hates you.
44 And I say to you, Love those hating you; bless those cursing you; do good to those hating you, and pray over those abusing you and pursuing you,
45 So that you may be children of your Father in heaven, because he causes his sun to rise on the evil and on the inherently good, and showers on the righteous and on the unrighteous.
46 Because if you love those loving you, what reward do you have? Do absolutely not even the tax collectors do the same?
47 And if you embrace your brothers only, what more than is required are you doing? Do the tax collectors absolutely not do the same?
48 You therefore be perfect even as your Father in heaven is perfect."

It is obvious in this sermon that Jesus was commenting on the law given to Moses.

Why?

What is Jesus' approach to Moses?

We can see here that Jesus is correcting abuses and misunderstandings of the law that had arisen in the teachings of the rabbis.

The phrase So, "you have heard it said" refers to the rabbinic perversions of the law and not the law itself. The older Dispensational interpreters viewed the Sermon on the Mount as purely Mosaic Law to be reinstituted during the millennium.

They likewise, then, saw Jesus as criticizing the law's modern misinterpreters. For these, when Jesus says "But I say unto you," He is not offering anything new; He is merely expounding ("restoring") the original meaning of Moses' law.

Jesus' treatment of the law in Matthew 5:21-48 is a new application of the Law of Moses in keeping with the over-arching law of love.

What is meant by the law of love?

When the demands that Jesus had made in this sermon are preserved; the remainder of Moses Law is abolished.

We can see also that Jesus proceeds from loving one's neighbour Leviticus.19:18; *"You shall not avenge nor cherish a grudge against the children of your people, but you shall love your neighbour as yourself; I am Jehovah."* To loving one's enemy.

However one understands the "hate" clause here, it remains that "loving one's enemy" is a principle not immediately evident in any exposition of Moses but we can see that Jesus extends the law's requirement. We need to remember and believe with all our hearts that Jesus is greater than Moses, and greater than the law itself.

We can see from the writings in the Gospel of Matthew that Jesus is presented as the new Moses, yet greater and with superior authority. And when Jesus actually treats the law He is not hesitant to appear so.

Matthew 5:17; *"Do not suppose that I came to loosen down the law or the prophets; I absolutely did not come to loosen down, but to fulfil."*

When Jesus says "I came" He speaks in reference to His Messianic mission. The phrase "the law and the prophets" refers to (OT) Scripture as a whole. The verbs "destroy" and "fulfil" (in Greek; katalusai, plerosai) are both telic, or purpose, infinitives. Jesus is addressing and clarifying the goal of His mission in relation to the Scriptures.

However, Jesus denies that He has come with cross-purposes to the law. He will not invalidate the Scriptures which God has given; He will allow them to stand, and their purpose will continue to be served.

Jesus is the fulfilment of all the expectations regarding David's and Abraham's Son, and He is the one who "fills full" all the promises made throughout Israel's history. Speak of Bethlehem, Galilee, the Messiah, and the King of Israel/the Jews, the suffering Servant of Jehovah, the Son of Man, or any of a host of other terms pregnant with expectation, and Jesus is the Fulfiller, the answer and goal of them all.

"The law and the prophets were until John; since that time the kingdom of God is preached, and every man presses into it. And it is easier for heaven and earth to pass, than one title of the law to

fall."

Again it is Jesus Himself who specifies that the law had a prophetic/prospective function; it anticipated Him who brought about its expectations. In doing so, the law did not "fall" The whole law, then, was taken up into Christ, and He gave to it its truest significance.

What that significance is, is for Him to explain by His teaching us personally John 16:12-13; *"I have yet many things to say to you, but you absolutely do not have power to bear them just now. But when he comes, the Spirit of truth, he will guide you into all truth, because he will absolutely not speak from himself, but whatever he hears he will speak, and he will announce to you the things to come."*

God's law comes to the church from the hands of Christ, the Lord of the law. Continuity with Moses there is, but Moses is no longer the centre of attention nor the final court of appeal: that prerogative belongs to One greater than Moses.

It is Jesus' teaching which forms the ultimate standard of righteousness and Who pronounces with supreme authority what is the will of God. He clarifies that righteousness which Moses' law only foreshadowed.

Colossians.2:17; *"Which are a shadow of things to come, and the body is of Christ."*

We can see clearly from this verse that Moses has stepped aside and given way to this One Who's teaching forms the ultimate standard of righteousness and Who pronounces with supreme authority what is the will of God. He clarifies that righteousness which Moses' law only foreshadowed.

What Jesus presents is not a re-ratified old covenant law, but a fulfilled law for a new era and a new covenant people. Thus, when the emphasis is taken off Moses and placed on to Christ. It is the law interpreted by Him which remains binding.

The Law and the Spirit of Life

Romans. 8; "*There is therefore now absolutely no condemnation to those in Christ Jesus, who do not walk according to the flesh, but according to the Spirit,*
2 Because the law of the Spirit of life in Christ Jesus has set me free from the law of sin and death,
3 Because what the law did not have the power to do, in that it was weak through the flesh, God sending his own Son in the likeness of sinful flesh, and for sin, condemned sin in the flesh,
4 That the righteous deeds of the law might be fulfilled in us, who walk not according to the flesh, but according to the Spirit,
5 Because they who are according to the flesh exercise their mind on the things of the flesh, and those according to the Spirit, on the things of the Spirit,
6 Because to be fleshly minded is death, but to be spiritually minded is life and peace.
7 On this very account the fleshly mind is hostile against God, because it absolutely will not arrange itself under the law of God, because it absolutely does not have the power.
8 And those being in the flesh absolutely do not have the power to please God.
9 But you are absolutely not in the flesh, but in the Spirit, if the Spirit of God is housed in you. And if anyone absolutely does not have the Spirit of Christ, he is absolutely none of his.
10 And if Christ is in you, truly the body is dead through sin, but the Spirit is life through righteousness.
11 And if the Spirit of him who raised up Jesus out of the dead is housed in you, he who raised up Christ out of the dead will also make your mortal bodies alive through his Spirit who is housed within you.
12 So therefore, brothers, we are debtors, absolutely not to the flesh to live according to the flesh,
13 Because if you live according to the flesh, of necessity you will die, but if through the Spirit you put to death the action of the body, you will live,
14 Because as many as are led by the Spirit of God, they are the children of God,
15 Because you have absolutely not taken the spirit of servitude again into fear, but you have taken the Spirit of adoption, in which we scream out, Abba, Father.
16 The Spirit himself witnesses with our spirit, that we are children of God,
17 And if children, also heirs; heirs truly of God, and joint-heirs with Christ; if it is that we suffer with him, then we will also be glorified together,
18 Because I calculate that the experiences of this present time are absolutely not worthy of the glory about to be revealed into us,
19 Because the earnest expectation of the creature is fully expecting the revelation of the children of God,
20 Because the creature was arranged under futile emptiness, absolutely not voluntarily, but through him who caused it to be arranged under him upon hope,
21 Because also the creature itself will be set free from the servitude to decay into the glorious liberty of the children of God,
22 Because we see that the whole creation groans and experiences birth pains together until now.
23 And absolutely not only they, but also ourselves, having the first fruits of the Spirit, we also ourselves sigh under pressure within ourselves, fully expecting the adoption, the redemption of our body,
24 Because we were saved by hope, but hope seen is not hope, because what anyone sees, why does he also hope?
25 And if we hope for what we absolutely do not see, through cheerful endurance we fully expect it.
26 And likewise the Spirit also takes hold with us of our weaknesses, because we absolutely do not see what we should pray as we should, but the Spirit himself intercedes for us with groanings which cannot be uttered.
27 And he who searches the hearts sees what is the mind of the Spirit, because according to God he intercedes for the saints.

28 And we see that all things work together into inherent good to them who love God, to them who are the called according to his purpose,
29 Because whom he foreknew he also predestined to be shaped like the image of his Son, into his being the firstborn among many brothers.
30 And whom he predestined, them he also called, and whom he called, them he also justified, and whom he justified, them he also glorified.
31 What therefore shall we speak to these things? If God is for us, who can be against us?
32 He who absolutely did not spare his own Son, but gave him up for us all, how will he absolutely not with him also grace us with all things?
33 Who will bring any charge against God's chosen? God is the one who justifies.
34 Who is he who condemns? Christ is the one who died, and more, is risen again, who is also in the right hand of God, who also intercedes for us.
35 Who shall separate us from the love of Christ? Tribulation, or distress, or persecution, or famine, or nakedness, or danger, or sword?
36 As it has been written, For your sake we are killed the whole day; we are calculated as sheep for the slaughter.
37 On the contrary, in all these things we are more than conquerors through him who loved us,
38 Because I am convinced, that absolutely not death, absolutely not life, absolutely not supernatural messengers, absolutely not head rulers, absolutely not powers, absolutely not things present, absolutely not things to come,
39 Absolutely not height, absolutely not depth, absolutely not any other creature, will have the power to separate us from the love of God which is in Christ Jesus our Lord."

In this scripture we can see that Paul presents to us in detail the positive side of life in the Spirit. "There is therefore now no condemnation", he begins, and this statement may at first seem out of place here.

Surely condemnation was met by the Blood through which we found peace with God and salvation from wrath.

Romans 5:1-9; *"Therefore having been justified out of faith, we have peace toward God through our Lord Jesus Christ,*
2 Through whom also we have had access by faith into this grace in which we stand, and boast upon hope of the glory of God.
3 And absolutely not only this, but we boast in tribulations also, seeing that tribulation fully works cheerful endurance;
4 And cheerful endurance, testing's, and testing's, hope;
5 And hope absolutely does not put us to shame, because the love of God is poured out in our hearts through the Holy Spirit given to us.
6 Because while we were yet without strength, in due time Christ died for the ungodly,
7 Because it is difficult for anyone to die for one righteous; some might dare to die for one inherently good.
8 And God caused his love to stand together toward us, in that, while we were yet sinners, Christ died for us.
9 Much more therefore, having been now justified in his blood, we shall be saved through him from wrath."

But there are two kinds of condemnation, namely, that before God and that before myself (just as earlier we saw there are two kinds of peace) and the second may at times seem to us even more awful than the first.

When I see that the Blood of Christ has satisfied God, then I know my sins are forgiven, and there is for me no more condemnation before God. Yet I may still know defeat, and the sense of inward condemnation on this account may be very real,

Romans 7; *"Or are you ignorant, brothers - because I speak to them who know the law - that the law lords it over a man over such time as he lives?*
2 Because the woman subject to a husband is bound by the law to the living husband, and in case the husband dies, she is rendered inoperative from the law of her husband.
3 So therefore if, the husband living, she is to another man, according to divine oracle she is an adulteress, and if the husband dies she is free from that law, so that, being to another man, she is not an adulteress.
4 Therefore, my brothers, you also were made dead to the law through the body of Christ, into becoming married to another, to the one raised out of the dead, that we may bear fruit to God,
5 Because when we were in the flesh, the experiences of sins, which were through the law, were supernaturally working in our members to bear the fruit of death.
6 And now we are rendered inoperative from the law, being dead in which we were held down; thus we serve in newness of spirit, and not in the oldness of the letter.
7 What therefore shall we speak? Is the law sin? It is not! On the contrary, I absolutely did not know sin except through the law; also because I absolutely did not see longing except the law said, You shall absolutely not set your passion on it.
8 And sin, taking a starting point through the commandment, completely worked in me all longings, because apart from law sin was dead.
9 And I was alive separate from law at one time, and when the commandment came sin revived, and I died.
10 And the commandment, which was into life, I found to be into death,
11 Because sin, taking a starting point through the commandment, deceived me, and through it killed me.
12 Therefore truly the law is holy, and the commandment holy, and righteous, and inherently good.
13 Did therefore the inherent good become death to me? It was not; but sin, that it might be manifest as sin, fully working death in me through the inherent good, that sin through the commandment might become pre-eminently sinful,
14 Because we see that the law is spiritual, and I am fleshly, having been sold under sin,
15 Because what I fully work, I absolutely do not know, because what I will, I absolutely do not practice, but what I hate, this I do.
16 And if I do this, what I absolutely do not will, I agree with the law that it is beautifully good.
17 And now it is absolutely no longer I fully working it, but sin being housed in me,
18 Because I see that in me - that is, in my flesh - is housed absolutely no inherent good, because to will is present with me, but how to fully work the beautifully good, I absolutely do not find,
19 Because the inherent good I will, I absolutely do not do, but the evil I absolutely do not will, that I practice.
20 And if what I absolutely do not will, that I do, it is absolutely no longer I that is fully working it, but sin being housed in me.
21 I find then the law: when I will to do the beautifully good, evil is present with me,
22 Because I delight in the law of God according to the inward man,
23 But I am looking at a different law in my members, warring against the law of my mind, and bringing me into captivity to the law of sin which is in my members.
24 I am a wretched man! Who will deliver me out of the body of this death?
25 I thank God through Jesus Christ our Lord. So therefore I myself indeed with the mind serve the law of God, but with the flesh, the law of sin."

We can see this in this scripture how we can still have the sense of inward condemnation and how real it is. But if I have learned to live by Christ as my life, then I have learned the secret of victory, and, praise God! "There is therefore now no condemnation". "The mind of the spirit is life and peace,"

Romans 8:6; *"Because to be fleshly minded is death, but to be spiritually minded is life and peace."*

And this becomes my experience as I learn to walk in the Spirit. With peace in my heart I have no time to feel condemned, but only to praise Him who leads me on from victory to victory.

But what lay behind my sense of condemnation?

Was it not the experience of defeat and the sense of helplessness to do anything about it?

Before I saw that Christ is my life, I laboured under a constant sense of handicap; limitation dogged my steps; I felt disabled at every turn. I was always crying out: 'I cannot do this! I cannot do that!' Try as I would, I found that I "cannot please God."

Romans 8:8; *"And those being in the flesh absolutely do not have the power to please God."*

But there we find ourselves saying no 'I cannot' in Christ. Now it is: "I can do all things in him that strengthened me."

Philippians. 4:13; *"I am strong for all things in Christ who empowers me."*

How can Paul be so daring?

On what ground does he declare that he is now free from limitation and "can do all things"?

Here is his answer: "For the law of the Spirit of life in Christ Jesus made me free from the law of sin and of death"

Romans 8:2; *"Because the law of the Spirit of life in Christ Jesus has set me free from the law of sin and death,"*

Why is there no more condemnation?

"For ..." there is a reason for it; there is something definite to account for it. The reason is that there is a law called "the law of the Spirit of life" and it has proved stronger than another law called 'the law of sin and death".

The three questions we will consider is:

1. What are these laws?

2. How do they operate?

3. And what is the difference between sin and the law of sin, and between death and the law of death?

First let us ask ourselves,

What is a law?

Well, strictly speaking, a law is a generalization examined until it is proved that there is no exception. We might define it more simply as something which happens over and over again. Each time the thing happens it happens in the same way.

We can illustrate this both from statutory and from natural law. For example, in this land, if I drive a car on the right hand side of the road the traffic police will stop me.

Why?

The answer is because it is against the law of the land. If you do it you will be stopped too.

Why?

For the same reason that I would be stopped: it is against the law and the law makes no exceptions. It is something which happens repeatedly and unfailingly.

Or again, we all know what is meant by gravity. If I drop my handkerchief in London it falls to the ground. That is the effect of gravity. But the same is true if I drop it in Berlin or Paris.

No matter where I let it go, gravity operates, and it always produces the same results. Whenever the same conditions prevail the same effects are seen. There is thus a 'law' of gravity.

Now what of the law of sin and death?

If someone passes an unkind remark about me, at once something goes wrong inside me. That is not law; that is sin. But it, when different people pass unkind remarks, the same 'something' goes wrong inside, then I discern a law within—a law of sin.

Like the law of gravity, it is something constant. It always works the same way. And it is the same too with the law of death.

Death, we have said, is weakness produced to its limit. Weakness is 'I cannot'. Now if when I try to please God in this particular matter I find I cannot and if when I try to please Him in that other thing I again find I cannot, then I discern a law at work.

There is not only sin in me but a law of sin; there is not only death in me but a law of death. Then again, not only is gravity a law in the sense that it is constant, admitting of no exception, but, unlike the rule of the road, it is a 'natural' law and not the subject of discussion and decision but of discovery.

The law is there, and the handkerchief 'naturally' drops by itself without any help from me. And the "law" discovered by the man in Romans 7:23 which says; *"Because the wages of sin is death, and the gift of God is eternal life in Christ Jesus our Lord."*

Is just like that. It is a law of sin and of death, opposed to that which is good, and crippling the man's will to do good. He 'naturally' sins according to the "law of sin" in his members.

He wills to be different, but that law in him is relentless and no human will can resist it.

So this brings me to the question,

How can I be set free from the law of sin and death?

I need deliverance from sin, and still more do I need deliverance from death, but most of all I need deliverance from the law of sin and of death.

How can I be delivered from the constant repetition of weakness and failure?

In order to answer this question let us follow out our two illustrations further. One of the great burdens in China used to be the liken tax, a law which no one could escape, originating from the China Dynasty and operating right down to our own day.

It was an inland tax on the transit of goods, applied throughout the empire and having numerous barriers for collection, and officers enjoying very large powers.

The result was that the charge on goods passing through several provinces might become very heavy indeed. But a few years ago a second law came into operation which set aside the liken law.

Can you imagine the feelings of relief in those who had suffered under the old law?

Now there was no need to think or hope or pray; the new law was already there and had delivered us from the old law. No longer was there need to think beforehand what one would say if one met a liken officer tomorrow!

And as with the law of the land, so it is with natural law.

How can the law of gravity be annulled?

With regard to my handkerchief that law is at work clearly enough, pulling it down, but I have only to place my hand under the handkerchief and it does not drop.

Why?

The law is still there. I do not deal with the law of gravity; in fact I cannot deal with the law of gravity.

Then why does my handkerchief not fall to the ground?

The answer is because there is a power keeping it from doing so. The law is there, but another law superior to it is operation to overcome it, namely the law of life.

Gravity can do its utmost but the handkerchief will not drop, because another law is working against the law of gravity to maintain it there. We have all seen the tree which was once a small seed fallen between the slabs of a paving, and which has grown until heavy stone blocks have been lifted by the power of the life within it. That is what we mean by the triumph of one law over another.

In just such a manner God delivers us from one law by introducing another law. The law of sin and death is there all the time, but God has put another law into operation - the law of the Spirit of life in Christ Jesus, and that law is strong enough to deliver us from the law of sin and death.

You see, it is a law of life in Christ Jesus—the resurrection life that in Him has met death in all its forms and triumphed over it.

Ephesians. 1:19-20; *"And what is the surpassing greatness of his power to us, those believing according to the supernatural working of the might of his strength, Which he supernaturally worked in Christ, raising him out of the dead, and he seated him in his right hand in the heavenlies,"*

The Lord Jesus dwells in our hearts in the person of His Holy Spirit, and if we let Him have a clear way and commit ourselves to Him we shall find that He will keep us from the old law. We shall learn what it is to be kept, not by our own power, but "by the power of God"

1 Peter 1:5; *"The ones guarded beforehand in the power of God through faith into salvation ready to be revealed in the last time."*

What is meant by the Manifestation of the Law of Life?

Let us seek to make this practical. We touched earlier on the matter of our will in relation to the things of God. Even older Christians do not realize how great a part will-power plays in their lives.

That was part of Paul's trouble as we have seen in Romans 7. His will was good, but all his actions contradicted it, and however much he made up his mind and set himself to please God, it led him only into worse darkness.

'I would do well', but "I am carnal, sold under sin". That is the point. Like a car without petrol, that has to be pushed and that stops as soon as it is left alone, many Christians endeavour to drive themselves by will-power, and then think the Christian life a most exhausting and bitter one.

Some even force themselves to say 'Hallelujah!' because others do it, while admitting there is no meaning in it to them. They force themselves to be what they are not, and it is worse than trying to make water run up-hill. For after all, the very highest point the will can reach is that of willingness.

Matthew. 26:41; *"Watch and pray lest you enter into temptation; indeed the spirit is passionately forward, but the flesh is weak."*

If we have to exert so much effort in our Christian living, it simply says that we are not really like that at all. We don't need to force ourselves to speak our native language.

In fact we only have to exert will-power in order to do things we do not do naturally. We may do them for a time, but the law of sin and death wins in the end.

We may be able to say: 'To will is present with me, and I perform that which is good for two weeks', but eventually we shall have to confess: 'How to perform it I know not'. No, what I already am I do not long to be. If I "would" it is because I am not.

There is another question that many Christians ask:

Why do men use will-power to try to please God?

There may be two reasons. They may of course never have experienced the new birth, in which case they have no new life to draw upon, or they may have been born again and the life be there, but they have not learned to trust in that life. It is this lack of understanding that results in habitual failure and sinning, bringing them to the place where they almost cease to believe in the possibility of anything better.

But because we have not believed fully, that does not mean that the feeble life we intermittently experience is all God has given us.

Romans 6:23 states that *"the free gift of God is eternal life in Christ Jesus our Lord"*, and now in Romans 8:2 we read that *"the law of the Spirit of life in Christ Jesus"* has come to our aid.

So Romans 8:2 speaks not of a new gift but of the life already referred to in Romans 6:23. In other words, it is a new revelation of what we already have.

I feel I cannot emphasize this too much.

It is not something fresh from God's hand, but a new unveiling of what He has already given. It is a new discovery of a work already done in Christ, for the words "made me free" are in the past tense. If I really see this and put my faith in Him, there is no absolute necessity for Romans 7 to be repeated in me, either the experience or the conduct, and certainly not the tremendous display of will-power.

If we will let go our own wills and trust Him, we shall not fall to the ground and break, but we shall fall into a different law, the law of the Spirit of life. For He has given us not only life; but a law of life; And just as the law of gravity is a natural law and not the result of human legislation, so the law of life is a 'natural' law, similar in principle to the law that keeps our heart beating or that controls the movement of our eyelids.

There is no need for us to think about our eyes, or to decide that we must blink every so often to keep them cleansed; and still less do we bring our will to bear upon our heart. Indeed to do so might rather harm than help it.

No, so long as it has life it works spontaneously. Our wills only interfere with the law of life. I discovered that fact once in the following way. When we look to sleep there are many of us who have difficulty in sleeping.

The reasons for this are that sleep is as much a law as hunger is, and I realized that though I had never thought of worrying whether I would get hungry or not, I had been worrying about sleeping.

I had been trying to help nature, and that is the chief trouble with most sufferers from sleeplessness. But now I trusted not only God but God's law of nature, and slept well.

Others would say that should we not read the Bible!

Of course we should or our spiritual life will suffer. But that should not mean forcing ourselves to read.

There is a new law in us which gives us a hunger for it. Then half an hour can be more profitable than five hours of forced reading. And it is the same with giving, with preaching, with testimony.

Forced preaching is apt to result in preaching a warm gospel with a cold heart, and we all know what men mean by 'cold charity'. If we will let ourselves live in the new law we shall be less conscious of the old law. It is still there, but it is no longer governing and we are no longer in its grip.

That is why the Lord says in Matthew 6: *"Behold the birds... Consider the lilies."*

If we could ask the birds whether they were not afraid of the law of gravity, **how would they reply?**

They would say: 'We never heard the name of Newton. We know nothing about his law. We fly because it is the law of our life to fly.'

Not only is there in them a life with the power of flight, but that life has a life has a law which enables these living creatures quite spontaneously and consistently to overcome the law of gravity.

Yet gravity remains. If you get up early one morning when the cold is intense and the snow thick on the ground, and there is a dead sparrow in the courtyard, you are reminded at once of the persistence of that law. But while birds live they overcome it, and the life within them is what dominates their consciousness.

God has been truly gracious to us. He has given us this new law of the Spirit and for us to 'fly' is no longer a question of our will but of His life.

Have you noticed what a trial it is to make an impatient Christian patient?

To require patience of him is enough to make him ill with depression. But God has never told us to force ourselves to be what we are not naturally: to try by taking thought to add to our spiritual stature.

Worrying may possibly decrease a man's height, but it certainly never added anything to it. "Be not anxious", are His words. *"Consider the lilies, ... they grow."* He is directing our attention to the new law of life in us. Oh, for a new appreciation of the life that is ours!

What a precious discovery this is! It can make altogether new men of us, for it operates in the smallest things as well as in the bigger ones. It checks us when, for example, we put out a hand to look at a book in someone else's room, reminding us that we have not asked permission and have no right to do so. We cannot, the Holy Spirit tells us, encroach thus upon the rights of others.

But the real question we need to ask ourselves is,

Have they the life of the Lord within?

For I tell you, that life can say to them: "Your voice is too loud", or, "That laughter was not right", or, "Your motive in passing that remark was wrong."

In a thousand details the Spirit of life can tell them how to act, so producing in them a true refinement. There is no such inherent power in education.' But it is true. Take the example of talkativeness.

Are you a person of too many words?

When you stay with people, do you say to yourself: 'What shall I do? I am a Christian; but if I am to glorify the name of the Lord, I simple must not talk so much. So today let me be extra careful to hold myself in check.'? And for an hour or two you succeed, until on some pretext you loose control and, before you know where you are, find yourself once again in difficulty with your garrulous tongue.

Yes, let us be fully assured that the will is useless here. For me to exhort you to exercise your will in this matter would be but to offer you the vain religion of the world, not the life in Christ Jesus.

To consider again: a talkative person remains just that, though he keep silent all day, for there is a 'natural' law of talkativeness governing him or her! Just as a peach tree is a peach tree whether or not it bears peaches or not is the same thing.

But as Christians we discover a new law in us, the law of the spirit of life, which transcends all else and which has already delivered us from the 'law' of our talkativeness.

If, believing the Lord's Word, we yield ourselves to that new law, it will tell us when we should stop talking, or not start! And it will empower us to do so.

On that basis you can go to your friend's house for two or three hours, or stay for two or three days, and experience no difficulty. On your return you will just thank God for His new law of life.
Amen

Calvin on the Law and the Gospel

This final chapter is to give you an understanding on Calvin on the Law and the Gospel. It is this spontaneous life that is the Christian life. It manifests itself in love for the unlovely, for the brother whom on natural grounds we would not like and certainly could not love.

It works on the basis of what the Lord sees of possibility in that brother. 'Lord, You see he is lovable and You love him. Love him, now, through me!' And it manifests itself in reality of life, in a true genuineness of moral character.

There is too much hypocrisy in the lives of Christians, too much play-acting. Nothing takes away from the effectiveness of Christian witness as does a pretence of something that is not really there, for the man in the street unfailingly penetrates such a disguise in the end and finds us out for what we are. Yes, pretence gives way to reality when we trust the law of life.

Since God was pleased to testify in ancient times by means of expiations and sacrifices that he was a Father, and to set apart for himself a chosen people, he was doubtless known even then in the same character in which he is now fully revealed to us.

Accordingly Malachi, having enjoined the Jews to attend to the Law of Moses because after his death there was to be an interruption of the prophetical office, immediately after declares that the Sun of righteousness should arise

Malachi 4:2; *"And to you who fear my name the Sun of Righteousness shall rise with healing in his wings, and you shall go forth, and spread out as calves of the stall."*

Thus intimating, that though the Law had the effect of keeping the pious in expectation of the coming Messiah, there was ground to hope for much greater light on his advent. For this reason, Peter, speaking of the ancient prophets, says in 1 Peter 1:12, *"Unto whom it was revealed, that not unto themselves, but unto us, they did minister the things which are now reported unto you by them that have preached the gospel unto you, with the Holy Ghost sent down from heaven."*

Not that the prophetical doctrine was useless to the ancient people, or unavailing to the prophets themselves, but that they did not obtain possession of the treasure which God has transmitted to us by their hands. They had only a slight foretaste; to us is given a fuller fruition.

Our Saviour, accordingly, while he declares that Moses testified of him, extols the superior measure of grace bestowed upon us.

John 5:46; *"Because if you were believing Moses, you were believing me, because that one wrote about me."*

Addressing his disciples, he says, "Blessed are your eyes, for they see, and your ears, for they hear. For verily I say unto you, That many prophets and righteous men have desired to see those things which ye see, and have not seen them, and to hear those things which ye hear, and have not heard them,"

Matthew 13:16; *"And blessed are your eyes, because they see, and your ears,because they hear."*

Luke 10:23; *"And having turned to his disciples, he said privately, Blessed are the eyes seeing what you see,"*

It is no small commendation of the gospel revelation, that God has preferred us to holy men of old, so much distinguished for piety. There is nothing in this view inconsistent with another passage, in which our Saviour says, "Your father Abraham rejoiced to see my day, and he saw it and was glad,"

John 8:56; *"Your father Abraham jumped for joy to see my day, and he saw, and rejoiced."*

Even though the event of this is remote, his view of it was obscure, he had full assurance that it would one day be accomplished; and hence the joy which the holy patriarch experienced even to his death.

Nor does John Baptist, when he says, "No man has seen God at any time; the only begotten Son, which is in the bosom of the Father, he has declared him,"

John 1:18; *"Absolutely no one has gazed at God at any time; the only begotten Son, who is into the bosom of the Father, he has brought him out."*

We see that he exclude the pious who had previously died from a participation in the knowledge and light which are manifested in the person of Christ; but comparing their condition with ours, he intimates that the mysteries which they only beheld dimly under shadows are made clear to us; as is well explained by the author of the Epistle to the Hebrews, in these words in Hebrews 1:1-2, *"God, who at sundry times and in divers manners spake in time past unto the fathers by the prophets, has in these last days spoken unto us by his Son,"*

Hence, although this only begotten Son, who is now to us the brightness of his Father's glory and the express image of his person, was formerly made known to the Jews, as we have elsewhere shown from Paul, that he was the Deliverer under the old dispensation; it is nevertheless true, as Paul himself elsewhere declares in 2 Corinthians 4:6, that *"God, who commanded the light to shine out of darkness, has shined in our hearts, to give the light of the knowledge of the glory of God in the face of Jesus Christ,"*; because, when he appeared in this his image, he in a manner made himself visible, his previous appearance having been shadowy and obscure.

More shameful and more detestable, therefore, is the ingratitude of those who walk blindfold in this meridian light. Accordingly,

Paul says in 2 Corinthians 4:4 that *"the god of this world has blinded their minds, lest the light of the glorious gospel of Christ should shine unto them."*

What is meant by the Gospel?

It means the clear manifestation of the mystery of Christ. In the sense that the term Gospel is applied by Paul to the doctrine of faith

2 Timothy 4:10; *"Because Demas has forsaken me, having loved this present world, and gone to Thessalonica, Crescens to Galatia, Titus to Dalmatia."*

It includes all the promises by which God reconciles men to himself, and which occur throughout the Law. Paul we see opposes faith to those terrors which vex and torment the conscience when salvation is sought by means of works.

Hence it follows that Gospel, taken in a large sense, comprehends the evidences of mercy and paternal favour which God bestowed on the Patriarchs. Still, by way of excellence, it is applied to the promulgation of the grace manifested in Christ. This is not only founded on general use, but has the sanction of our Saviour and his Apostles.

Therefore it is described as one of his peculiar characteristics, that he preached the Gospel of the kingdom.

Matthew 4:23; *"And Jesus went around the whole of Galilee, teaching in their synagogues, and preaching the good news of the kingdom, and healing every sickness and every weakness in the people."*

Matthew 9:35; *"And Jesus went around all the cities and villages teaching in their synagogues, and preaching the good news of the kingdom, and healing every sickness and every weakness in the people."*

Mark 1:14; *"And after that John was given over into prison, Jesus came into Galilee, preaching the good news of the kingdom of God,"*

Mark, in his preface to the Gospel, calls it "The beginning of the Gospel of Jesus Christ."

There is no use of collecting passages to prove what is already perfectly known. Christ at his advent "brought life and immortality to light through the Gospel,"

2 Timothy 1:10' *"And is now manifest through the appearing of our Saviour, Jesus Christ, who has truly rendered death inoperative, and has brought life and incorruptibility to light through the good news,"*

Paul does not mean by these words that the Fathers were plunged in the darkness of death before the Son of God became incarnate; but he claims for the Gospel the honourable distinction of being a new and extraordinary kind of embassy, by which God fulfilled what he had promised, these promises being realised in the person of the Son.

For though believers have at all times experienced the truth of Paul's declaration, that "all the promises of God in him are yea and amen," inasmuch as these promises were sealed upon their hearts; yet because he has in his flesh completed all the parts of our salvation, this vivid manifestation of realities was justly entitled to this new and special distinction.

Accordingly, Christ says, "Hereafter ye shall see heaven open, and the angels of God ascending and descending upon the Son of man." For though he seems to allude to the ladder which the Patriarch Jacob saw in vision, he commends the excellence of his advent in this, that it opened the gate of heaven, and gave us familiar access to it.

Here we must guard against the l imagination of Servetus, who, from a wish, or at least the pretence of a wish, to extol the greatness of Christ, abolishes the promises entirely, as if they had come to an end at the same time with the Law.

He pretends that by the faith of the Gospel all the promises have been fulfilled; as if there was no distinction between us and Christ. I lately observed that Christ had not left any part of our salvation incomplete; but from this it is erroneously inferred, that we are now put in possession of all the blessings purchased by him; thereby implying, that Paul was incorrect in saying in Romans 3:24, "*We are saved by hope.*"

However by believing in Christ we pass from death unto life; but we must at the same time remember the words of John, that though we know we are "the sons of God," "it does not yet appear what we shall be: but we know that, when he shall appear, we shall be like him; for we shall see him as he is,"

1 John 3:2; *"Beloved, now we are the children of God, and it absolutely does not yet appear what we shall be, but we see that, when he appears, we shall be like him, because we shall see him as he is."*

Therefore, although Christ offers us in the Gospel a present fullness of spiritual blessings, fruition remains in the keeping of hope, as in French it is written, "sous la garde, et comme sous le cachet d'espoir;" under the guard, and as it were, under the seal of hope.

Until we are divested of corruptible flesh, and transformed into the glory of him who has gone before us. Meanwhile, in leaning on the promises, we obey the command of the Holy Spirit, whose authority ought to have weight enough with us to silence all the barking of that impure dog.

We have it on the testimony of Paul, that "Godliness is profitable unto all things, having promise of the life that now is, and of that which is to come,"

1 Timothy 4:8; *"Because bodily exercise is a little advantageous, and godliness is advantageous to all things, having promise of the life now, and the one about to be."*

For which reason, he glories in being "an apostle of Jesus Christ, according to the promise of life which is in Christ Jesus."

2 Timothy 1:1; *"Paul, an apostle of Jesus Christ, through the will of God, according to the promise of life in Christ Jesus:"*

And he elsewhere reminds us, that we have the same promises which were given to the saints in ancient time.

2 Corinthians 7:1; *"Therefore having these promises, beloved, let us cleanse ourselves from all defilements of the flesh and spirit, completing holiness in the fear of God."*

In fine, he makes the sum of our felicity consist in being sealed with the Holy Spirit of promise. Indeed we have no enjoyment of Christ, unless by embracing him as clothed with his own promises. Hence it is that he indeed dwells in our hearts and yet we are as pilgrims in regard to him, because "we walk by faith, not by sight,"

2 Corinthians 5:6-7; *"Therefore being encouraged always, also seeing that, being at home in the body, we are absent from the Lord, Because we walk through faith, absolutely not through appearance;"*

There is no inconsistency in the two things that in Christ we possess every thing pertaining to the perfection of the heavenly life, and yet that faith is only a vision "of things not seen,"

Hebrews 11:1; *"And faith is the essence of things hoped for, the conviction of things absolutely not seen."*

Only there is this difference to be observed in the nature or quality of the promises that the Gospel points with the finger to what the Law shadowed under types.

Therefore we see the error of those who, in comparing the Law with the Gospel, represent it merely as a comparison between the merit of works, and the gratuitous imputation of righteousness.

The contrast thus made is by no means to be rejected, because, by the term Law, Paul frequently understands that rule of holy living in which God exacts what is his due, giving no hope of life unless we obey in every respect; and, on the other hand, denouncing a curse for the slightest failure.

This Paul does when showing that we are freely accepted of God, and accounted righteous by being pardoned, because that obedience of the Law to which the reward is promised is nowhere to be found.

Hence he appropriately represents the righteousness of the Law and the Gospel as opposed to each other. But the Gospel has not succeeded the whole Law in such a sense as to introduce a different method of salvation. It rather confirms the Law, and proves that every thing which it promised is fulfilled.

What was shadow, it has now made substance. When Christ says that the Law and the Prophets were until John, he does not consign the fathers to the curse, which, as the slaves of the Law, they could not escape.

He intimates that they were only imbued with the rudiments, and remained far beneath the height of the Gospel doctrine. Accordingly Paul, after calling the Gospel "the power of God unto salvation to every one that believeth," shortly after adds, that it was "witnessed by the Law and the Prophets,"

Romans 1:16; *"Because I am absolutely not ashamed of the good news of Christ, because it is the power of God into salvation to everyone who believes, both to the Jew first, also to the Greek,"*

Romans 3:21; *"And now the righteousness of God apart from the law has been manifested, being witnessed by the law and the prophets."*

And in the end of the same Epistle, though he describes "the preaching of Jesus Christ" as "the revelation of the mystery which was kept secret since the world began," he modifies the expression by adding, that it is "now made manifest" "by the scriptures of the prophets,"

Romans 16:25-26; *"And to the one having power to set you steadfast according to my good news, and the preaching of Jesus Christ, according to the revelation of the mystery, having been kept silent since the eternal ages, And now is made manifest, and through the Scriptures of the prophets, according to the decree of the everlasting God, made known to all races for the attentive hearing of faith,"*

Hence when the whole Law is spoken of, the Gospel differs from it only in respect of clearness of manifestation. Still, on account of the inestimable riches of grace set before us in Christ, there is good reason for saying, that by his advent the kingdom of heaven was erected on the earth.

Matthew 12.28; *"And if I throw out demons in the Spirit of God, then the kingdom of God has already arrived upon you."*

John stands between the Law and the Gospel, holding an intermediate office allied to both. For though he gave a summary of the Gospel when he pronounced Christ to be *"the Lamb of God who taketh away the sin of the world,"* yet, inasmuch as he did not unfold the incomparable power and glory which shone forth in his resurrection, Christ says that he was not equal to the Apostles. For this is the meaning of the words in Matthew. 11:28: *"Among them that are born of woman, there has not risen a greater than John the Baptist: notwithstanding, he that is least in the kingdom of heaven is greater than he,"*

He is not there commending the persons of men, but after preferring John to all the Prophets, he gives the first place to the preaching of the Gospel, which is elsewhere designated by the kingdom of heaven.

When John himself, in answer to the Jews, says that he is only "a voice,"

John 1:23; *"He said, I am a voice shouting in the wasteland, Make straight the way of the Lord, as the prophet Isaiah said."*

It is as if he were inferior to the Prophets it is not in pretended humility but he means to teach that the proper embassy was not entrusted to him, that he only performed the office of a messenger, as had been foretold by Malachi 4:5, *"Behold, I will send you Elijah the prophets before the coming of the great and dreadful day of the Lord,"*

And, indeed, during the whole course of his ministry, he did nothing more than prepare disciples for Christ. He even proves from Isaiah that this was the office to which he was divinely appointed.

In this sense, he is said by Christ to have been in John 5:35 *"a burning and a shining light,"*, because full day had not yet appeared. And yet this does not prevent us from classing him among the preachers of the gospel, since he used the same baptism which was afterwards committed to the Apostles.

Still, however, he only began that which had freer course under the Apostles, after Christ was taken up into the heavenly glory.

However with regards to the legal promises which the Lord proclaimed to the observers of the law, and they ask us whether we hold them to be null or effectual. Since it was absurd and ridiculous to say they are null, they take it for granted that they have some efficacy.

Hence they infer that we are not justified by faith only. For the Lord thus speaks in Deuteronomy 7:12-13: *"Wherefore it shall come to pass, if ye hearken to these judgments, and keep and do them, that the Lord thy God shall keep unto thee the covenant and the mercy which he sware unto thy fathers; and he will love thee, and bless thee and multiply thee,"*

Again in Jeremiah. 7:5-7, *"If ye thoroughly amend your ways and your doings; if ye thoroughly execute judgment between a man and his neighbour; if ye oppress not the stranger, the fatherless, and the widow, and shed not innocent blood in this place, neither walk after other gods to your hurt: then will I cause you to dwell in this place, in the land that I gave to your fathers, for ever and ever,"*

It was to no purpose to quote a thousand similar passages, which, as they are not different in meaning, are to be explained on the same principle. In substance, Moses declares that in the law is set down in Deuteronomy 11:26 *"a blessing and a curse,"* life and death; and hence they argue, either that that blessing is become inactive and unfruitful, or that justification is not by faith only.

The Lord does not promise any thing except to the perfect observers of the law; and none such are any where to be found. The results therefore is that the whole human race is convicted by the law, and exposed to the wrath and curse of God: to be saved from this they must escape from the power of the law, and be as it were brought out of bondage into freedom, not that carnal freedom which indisposes us for the observance of the law, tends to licentiousness, and allows our passions to wanton unrestrained with loosened reins.

But that spiritual freedom which consoles and raises up the alarmed and smitten conscience, proclaiming its freedom from the curse and condemnation under which it was formerly held bound. This freedom from subjection to the law, this manumission, if I may so express it, we obtain when by faith we apprehend the mercy of God in Christ, and are thereby assured of the pardon of sins, with a consciousness of which the law stung and tortured us.

Therefore the promises offered in the law would all be null and ineffectual, did not God in his goodness send the gospel to our aid, since the condition on which they depend, and under which only they are to be performed.

The fulfilment of the law will never be accomplished. Still, however the aid which the Lord gives consists not in leaving part of justification to be obtained by works, and in supplying part out of his indulgence, but in giving us Christ as in himself alone the fulfilment of righteousness.

For the Apostle, after premising that he and the other Jews, aware that "a man is not justified by the works of the law," had "believed in Jesus Christ," adds as the reason, not that they might be assisted to make up the sum of righteousness by faith in Christ, but that they "might be justified by the faith of Christ, and not by the works of the law,"

Galatians 2:16; *"Having seen that a man is absolutely not justified out of law works, but through Jesus Christ's faith, we also have believed into Jesus Christ, so that we may be justified out of Christ's faith, and absolutely not out of law works, because out of law works absolutely no flesh will be justified."*

If believers withdraw from the law to faith that in the latter they may find the justification which they see is not in the former they certainly disclaim justification by the law.

Therefore, whose will, let him amplify the rewards which are said to await the observer of the law, provided he at the same time understand, that owing to our depravity, we derive no benefit from them until we have obtained another righteousness by faith.

Thus David after making mention of the reward which the Lord has prepared for his servants for in Psalm 25; *"To you, Oh Jehovah, I lift up my soul.*
2 Oh my God, I trust in you; let me not pale in shame; do not let those who hate me jump for joy over me.
3 Yes, let none pale in shame who bind themselves to you; let them pale in shame who act deceitfully without cause.
4 Cause me to know by seeing your ways, Oh Jehovah; teach me your paths.
5 Cause me to tread in your truth, and teach me, because you are the God of my salvation; I bind myself to you all the day.
6 Remember, Oh Jehovah, your compassions, and your mercy, because they are forever.
7 Do not remember the sins of my youth and my transgressions; remember me according to your mercy, for your goodness' sake, Oh Jehovah.
8 Jehovah is good and straight; therefore he will cause sinners to flow into the way.
9 He will cause the meek to tread victoriously in judgment, and he will teach the meek his way.
10 All the paths of Jehovah are mercy and truth to those who guard his covenant and his testimonies.
11 Oh Jehovah, forgive my iniquity for your name's sake, because it is great.
12 Who is this, the man who fears Jehovah? He shall cause him to flow in the way he shall choose.

13 His soul shall dwell in good, and his seed shall inherit the earth.
14 The assembled counsel of Jehovah is with them who fear him; and he will cause them to know by seeing his covenant.
15 My eyes are continuously toward Jehovah, because he shall cause my feet to go out of the net.
16 Face around to me, and stoop down in grace to me, because I am alone and poor.
17 The pressures of my heart are broadened; Oh bring me out of my distresses.
18 See my affliction and my wearisome toil, and lift all my sins.
19 See those who hate me, because they are many, and they hate me with violent hate.
20 Hedge about my soul, and snatch me out; do not let me pale in shame, because I flee to you for refuge.
21 Let completeness and right guard me, because I am bound together with you.
22 Redeem Israel, Oh God, out of all his pressures."

We see that he immediately descends to an acknowledgment of sins, by which the reward is made void.

In Psalm 19; *"The heavens tally up the heavy glory of God, and the firmament causes the work of his hands to stand out boldly.*
2 Day to day gushes forth what he says, and night to night causes knowledge to live.
3 There is no speech, and there are no words where their voice is not heard.
4 Their measuring line is gone out through all the earth, and their discourse to the end of the inhabited earth. He has put a tent for the sun in them;
5 He is as a bridegroom coming out of his canopy, and will rejoice as a mighty man to run a path.
6 From the extremity of the heavens is his going forth, and his revolution to the ends of it, and there is nothing hid from his heat.
7 The law of Jehovah is complete, converting the soul; the testimony of Jehovah is faithful, making the open wise.
8 The visited mandates of Jehovah are straight, rejoicing the heart; the commandment of Jehovah is clean, lighting the eyes.
9 The fear of Jehovah is clean, standing forever; the judgments of Jehovah are nurturing and righteous as a unit.
10 More to be desired than gold, yes, than much fine gold, and sweeter than honey, and the dripping of honey from the comb.
11 Also your servant is enlightened by them, and in hedging them about there is great reward.
12 Who can understand his errors? From the hidden you cleanse me.
13 Also restrain your servant from arrogance; let them not rule over me; then I shall be complete, and I shall be clean from the great transgression.
14 Let the sayings of my mouth, and the murmurings of my heart, be pleasing before your face, Oh Jehovah, my strong rock, and my redeemer."

We also see that he loudly extols the benefits of the law; but immediately exclaims in Psalms. 19:12, *"Who can understand his errors? Cleanse thou me from secret faults,"*

This passage perfectly accords with the former, when, after saying, "the paths of the Lord are mercy and truth unto such as keep his covenant and his testimonies," he adds in Psalms 25:10-11, *"For thy name's sake, O Lord, pardon mine iniquity: for it is great,"*

Thus, too, we ought to acknowledge that the favour of God is offered to us in the law, provided by our works we can deserve it; but that it never actually reaches us through any such desert.

What then were the promises given that they might vanish away without fruit?

The Apostle shows, that the celebrated promise, "Ye shall therefore keep my statutes and my judgments: which if a man do, he shall live in them,"

Galatians 3:12; *"And the law is absolutely not out of faith, but, The man doing them shall live in them."*

Leviticus 18:5; *"You shall, therefore, hedge about my enactments and my judgments, in order that a man may do and live in them; I am Jehovah."*

When the gospel promises are substituted, promises which announce the free pardon of sins, the result is not only that our persons are accepted of God, but his favour also is shown to our works, and that not only in respect that the Lord is pleased with them, but also because he visits them with the blessings which were due by agreement to the observance of his law.

Therefore, the works of the faithful are rewarded with the promises which God gave in his law to the cultivators of righteousness and holiness; but in this reward we should always attend to the cause which procures favour to works.

This cause, then, appears to be threefold.

First, God turning his eye away from the works of his servants which merit reproach more than praise, embraces them in Christ, and by the intervention of faith alone reconciles them to himself without the aid of works.

Secondly the works not being estimated by their own worth, he, by his fatherly kindness and indulgence, honours so far as to give them some degree of value.

Thirdly, he extends his pardon to them, not imputing the imperfection by which they are all polluted, and would deserve to be regarded as vices rather than virtues.

Accordingly, of the three causes of divine liberality to which it owes that good works are accepted, they attended only to one: the other two, though the principal causes, they suppressed.

They quote the saying of Peter as given by Luke in the Acts 10:34- 35, *"Of a truth I perceive that God is no respecter of persons: but in every nation he that feareth him, and worketh righteousness, is accepted with him"*

And hence they infer, as a thing which seems to them beyond a doubt, that if man by right conduct procures the favour of God, his obtaining salvation is not entirely the gift of God. When God in his mercy assists the sinner, he is inclined to mercy by works.

There is no way of reconciling the passages of Scripture, unless you observe that man's acceptance with God is twofold. As man is by nature, God finds nothing in him which can incline him to mercy, except merely big wretchedness.

If it is clear then that man, when God first interposes for him, is naked and destitute of all good, and, on the other hand, loaded and filled with all kinds of evil, for what quality, pray, shall we say that he is worthy of the heavenly kingdom!

Where God thus clearly displays free mercy, have done with that empty imagination of merit.

Another passage in the same book where Cornelius hears from the lips of an angel in Acts 10:4, *"Thy prayer and thine alms are come up for a memorial before God,"* is miserably wrested to prove that man is prepared by the study of good works to receive the favour of God.

Cornelius being endued with true wisdom, in other words, with the fear of God, must have been enlightened by the Spirit of wisdom, and being an observer of righteousness, must have been sanctified by the same Spirit; righteousness being, as the Apostle testifies, one of the most certain fruits of the Spirit

Galatians 5:5; *"Because we by the Spirit fully expect the hope of righteousness out of faith,"*

Therefore, all those qualities by which he is said to have pleased God he owed to divine grace: so far was he from preparing himself by his own strength to receive it.

Indeed, not a syllable of Scripture can be produced which does not accord with the doctrine, that the only reason why God receives man into his favour is, because he sees that he is in every respect lost when left to himself; lost, if he does not display his mercy in delivering him.

We now see that in thus accepting, God looks not to the righteousness of the individual, but merely manifests the divine goodness towards miserable sinners, who are altogether undeserving of this great mercy. But after the Lord has withdrawn the sinner from the abyss of perdition, and set him apart for himself by means of adoption, having begotten him again and formed him to newness of life, he embraces him as a new creature, and bestows the gifts of his Spirit.

This is the acceptance to which Peter refers, and by which believers after their calling are approved by God even in respect of works; for the Lord cannot but love and delight in the good qualities which he produces in them by means of his Spirit. But we must always bear in mind, that the only way in which men are accepted of God in respect of works is, that whatever good works he has conferred upon those whom he admits to favour, he by an increase of liberality honours with his acceptance.

For whence their good works, but just that the Lord having chosen them as vessels of honour, is pleased to adorn them with true purity!

And how are their actions deemed good as if there was no deficiency in them, but just that their merciful Father indulgently pardons the spots and blemishes which adhere to them!

In one word, the only meaning of acceptance in this passage is that God accepts and takes pleasure in his children, in whom he sees the traces and lineaments of his own countenance. We have else here said that regeneration is a renewal of the divine image in us.

Since God, therefore, whenever he beholds his own face, justly loves it and holds it in honour, the life of believers, when formed to holiness and justice, is said, not without cause, to be pleasing to him. But because believers, while encompassed with mortal flesh, are still sinners, and their good works only begun savour of the corruption of the flesh, God cannot be propitious either to their persons or their works, unless he embraces them more in Christ than in themselves.

In this way are we to understand the passages in which God declares that he is clement and merciful to the cultivators of righteousness. Moses said to the Israelites, "Know, therefore, that the Lord thy God, he is God, the faithful God, which keepeth covenant and mercy with them that love him and keep his commandments, to a thousand generations."

These words afterwards became a common form of expression among the people. Thus Solomon in his prayer at the dedication says in 1 Kings 8:23, *"Lord God of Israel, there is no God like thee, in heaven above, or on earth beneath, who keepest covenant and mercy with thy servants that walk before thee with all their heart,"*

The same words are repeated by Nehemiah 1:5; *"And said, Oh please, now, Oh Jehovah God of the heavens, the great and terrible God, who hedges about covenant and mercy for them who love him and hedge about his commandments."*

Lord in all covenants of mercy stipulates on his part for integrity and holiness of life in his servants.

Deuteronomy 29:18; *"Lest there should stand among you man, or woman, or family, or tribe, whose heart faces about this day from Jehovah, our God, to walk to serve the gods of these peoples, lest there should be among you a root that bears a head of poison and wormwood;"*

Lest his goodness might be held in derision, or any one, puffed up with exultation in it, might speak flatteringly to his soul while walking in the depravity of his heart, so he is pleased that in this way those whom he admits to communion in the covenant should be kept to their duty.

However, the covenant was gratuitous at first, and such it ever remains. Accordingly, while David declares in 2 Samuel 22:20-21, *"according to the cleanness of my hands has he recompensed me," yet does he not omit the fountain to which I have referred; "he delivered me, because he delighted in me,"*

In commending the goodness of his cause, he derogates in no respect from the free mercy which takes precedence of all the gifts of which it is the origin.

What does it mean by legal promises?

By legal promises, I mean not those which lie scattered in the books of Moses for there many Evangelical promises occur, but those which properly belong to the legal dispensation. All such promises, by whatever name they may be called, are made under the condition that the reward is to be paid on the things commanded being done.

But when it is said that the Lord keeps a covenant of mercy with those who love him, the words rather demonstrate what kind of servants those are who have sincerely entered into the covenant, than express the reason why the Lord blesses them.

The nature of the demonstration is this: As the end for which God bestows upon us the gift of eternal life is, that he may be loved, feared, and worshipped by us, so the end of all the promises of mercy contained in Scripture justly is that we may reverence and serve their author.

Therefore, whenever we hear that he does good to those that observe his law, let us remember that the sons of God are designated by the duty which they ought perpetually to observe, that his reason for adopting us is, that we may reverence him as a father.

Hence, if we would not deprive ourselves of the privilege of adoption, we must always strive in the direction of our calling. On the other hand, however, let us remember, that the completion of the Divine mercy depends not on the works of believers, but that God himself fulfil the promise of salvation to those who by right conduct correspond to their calling, because he recognizes the true badges of sons in those only who are directed to good by his Spirit.

To this we may refer what is said of the members of the Church in Psalms 15:1-2 David says, *"Lord, who shall abide in thy tabernacle? Who shall dwell in thy holy hill? He that walketh uprightly, and worketh righteousness, and speaketh the truth in his heart,"*

Again, in Isaiah 33:14-15, "*Who among us shall dwell with the devouring fire? Who among us shall dwell with everlasting burnings? He that walketh righteously,"*

For the thing described is not the strength with which believers can stand before the Lord, but the manner in which our most merciful Father introduces them into his fellowship, and defends and confirms them therein.

For as he detests sin and loves righteousness, so those whom he unites to himself he purifies by his Spirit, that he may render them conformable to himself and to his kingdom.

Therefore, if one asks,

What is the first cause which gives the saints free access to the kingdom of God, and a firm and permanent footing in it?

The answer is easy. The Lord in his mercy once adopted and ever defends them. But if the question relates to the manner, we must descend to regeneration and the fruits of it, as enumerated Psalm 15; which says; *"Jehovah, who shall abide in your tent? Who shall dwell in your holy hill?*
2 He who walks complete in truth, and does the right, and speaks the truth in his heart,
3 He who does not walk as a spy with his tongue, does not do evil to his neighbour, does not lift up a reproach against his neighbour,
4 In whose eyes the despiser is despised, and he attributes heavy glory to them who fear Jehovah, he who swears to his own hurt, and does not exchange it;
5 He does not give out his silver on stinging interest, and does not take gifts against the innocent. He who does these shall never waver."

There seems much more difficulty in those passages which distinguish good works by the name of righteousness, and declare that man is justified by them.

The passages of the former class are very numerous, as when the observance of the commandments is termed justification or righteousness. Of the other classes we have a description in the words of Moses in Deuteronomy 6:25, *"It shall be our righteousness, if we observe to do all these commandments,"*

But if you object, that it is a legal promise, which, having an impossible condition annexed to it, proves nothing, there are other passages to which the same answer cannot be made; for instance in Deuteronomy 24:13, *"If the man be poor," "thou shalt deliver him the pledge again when the sun goes down:" "and it shall be righteousness unto thee before the Lord thy God,"*

Likewise we can see the same with the words of the prophet in Psalm 106:30-31, *"Then stood up Phinehas, and executed judgment: and so the plague was stayed. And that was counted unto him for righteousness unto all generations for evermore,"*

Accordingly the Pharisees of our day think they have here full scope for exultation. In French we hear the phrase, "de crier contre nous en cette endroit;" here to raise an outcry against us.

For, as we say, that when justification by faith is established, justification by works falls; they argue on the same principle, If there is a justification by works, it is false to say that we are justified by faith only.

When I grant that the precepts of the law are termed righteousness, I do nothing strange: for they are so in reality. But I readily give up any dispute as to the word. Nor do I deny that the Law of God contains a perfect righteousness.

For although we are debtors to do all the things which it enjoins, and, therefore, even after a full obedience, are unprofitable servants; yet, as the Lord has deigned to give it the name of righteousness, it is not ours to take from it what he has given.

We readily admit, therefore, that the perfect obedience of the law is righteousness, and the observance of any precept a part of righteousness, the whole substance of righteousness being contained in the remaining parts. But we deny that any such righteousness ever exists.

Hence we discard the righteousness of the law, not as being in itself maimed and defective, but because of the weakness of our flesh it nowhere appears. But then Scripture does not merely call the precepts of the law righteousness, it also gives this name to the works of the saints: as when it states that Zacharias and his wife in Luke 1:6 *"were both righteous before God, walking in all the commandments and ordinances of the Lord blameless,"*

Surely when it thus speaks, it estimates works more according to the nature of the law than their own proper character. The things contained in the law God enjoined upon man for righteousness but that righteousness we attain not unless by observing the whole law: every transgression whatever destroys it. While, therefore, the law commands nothing but righteousness, if we look to itself, every one of its precepts is righteousness: if we look to the men by whom they are performed, being transgressors in many things, they by no means merit the praise of righteousness for one work, and that a work which, through the imperfection adhering to it, is always in some respect vicious.

The French here adds the two following sentences: "Notre réponse donné est, mérités: mais entant qu'elles tendent à la justice que Dieu nous a commande, laquelle est nulle, si elle n'est parfaite. Or elle ne se trouve parfaite en nul homme de monde; pourtant faut conclure, qu'un bonne œuvre de soie ne mérité pas le nom de justice."

Our reply then is, that when the works of the saints are called righteousness, it is not owing to their merits, but is in so far as they tend to the righteousness which God has commanded, and which is null if it be not perfect. Now it is not found perfect in any man in the world.

Hence we must conclude that no good work merits in itself the name of righteousness.

What is justification?

Justification is defined as: The sinner being admitted into communion with Christ is, for his sake, reconciled to God; when purged by his blood he obtains the remission of sins, and clothed with righteousness, just as if it were his own, stands secure before the judgment-seat of heaven.

Forgiveness of sins being previously given, the good works which follow have a value different from their merit, because whatever is imperfect in them is covered by the perfection of Christ, and all their blemishes and pollutions are wiped away by his purity, so as never to come under the cognizance of the divine tribunal.

The guilt of all transgressions, by which men are prevented from offering God an acceptable service, being thus effaced, and the imperfection which is wont to sully even good works being buried, the good works which are done by believers are deemed righteous, or; which is the same thing, are imputed for righteousness.

However a question to be asked is:

How, then, will it appear to that eye before which even the heavens are not clean, and angels are chargeable with folly?

Job 4:18; *"Behold, he put no trust in his servants, and he charged his heavenly messengers with folly;"*

Thus he will be forced to confess that no good work exists that is not defiled, both by contrary transgression and also by its own corruption, so that it cannot be honoured as righteousness. But if it is certainly owing to justification by faith that works, otherwise impure, unclean, defective, unworthy of the sight, not to say of the love of God, are imputed for righteousness,

Why do they by boasting of this imputation aim at the destruction of that justification, but for which the boast were vain?

Are they desirous of having a viper's birth?

Would we have a viperfish progeny, where the children murder the parent?

To this their ungodly language tends. They cannot deny that justification by faith is the beginning, the foundation, the cause, the subject, the substance, of works of righteousness, and yet they conclude that justification is not by faith, because good works are counted for righteousness.

Let us have done then with this frivolity, and confess the fact as it stands; if any righteousness which works are supposed to possess depends on justification by faith, this doctrine is not only not impaired, but on the contrary confirmed, its power being thereby more brightly displayed.

Nor let us suppose, that after free justification works are commended, as if they afterwards succeeded to the office of justifying, or shared the office with faith. For justification by faith always remains entire, the impurity of works would be disclosed.

There is nothing absurd in the doctrine, that though man is justified by faith, he is himself only not righteous, but the righteousness attributed to his works is beyond their own deserts. In this way we can admit not only that there is a partial righteousness in works as our adversaries maintain, but that they are approved by God as if they were absolutely perfect.

If we remember on what foundation this is rested, every difficulty will be solved. The first time when a work begins to be acceptable is when it is received with pardon. And whence pardon, but just because God looks upon us and all that belongs to us as in Christ.

Therefore, as we ourselves when engrafted into Christ appear righteous before God, because our iniquities are covered with his innocence; so our works are, and are deemed righteous, because every thing otherwise defective in them being buried by the purity of Christ is not imputed.

Thus we may justly say, that not only ourselves, but our works also, are justified by faith alone.

Now, if that righteousness of works, whatever it be, depends on faith and free justification, and is produced by it, it ought to be included under it and, so to speak, made subordinate to it, as the effect to its cause; so far is it from being entitled to be set up to impair or destroy the doctrine of justification.

Now, if this righteousness of works, such as it is, proceeds from faith and free of justification. It must not be employed to destroy or obscure the grace on which it depends, but should rather be included in it, like the fruit in the tree.

Thus Paul, to prove that our blessedness depends not on our works, but on the mercy of God, makes special use of the words of David, "Blessed is he whose transgression is forgiven, whose sin is covered;" "Blessed is the man unto whom the Lord imputeth not iniquity."

Should any one here obtrude the numberless passages in which blessedness seems to be attributed to works, as, "Blessed is the man that feareth the Lord;" "He that has mercy on the poor, happy is he;" "Blessed is the man that walketh not in the counsel of the ungodly," and "that endureth temptation;" "Blessed are they that keep judgment," that are "pure in heart," "meek," "merciful,"

Romans 4:7; *"And if the truth of God has super-abounded in my falsehood into his glory, why am I yet also judged as a sinner?"*

Psalm 32:1-2; *"Blessed is the one whose transgression is lifted, whose sin is covered. Blessed is the man to whom Jehovah does not calculate iniquity, and in whose spirit there is no treachery."*

Psalm 112:1; *"Boast in Jehovah. Righteously happy is the man fearing Jehovah; he delights in his commandments exceedingly."*

Proverbs 14:21; *"He who despises his neighbour sins, and he who stoops down in grace to the meek, he is righteously happy."*

Psalm 1:1; *"Oh the righteous happiness's that are to the man who walks not in the counsel of the ungodly, nor stands in the way of sinners, nor sits in the seat of the scornful."*

Psalm 106:3; *"Righteously happy are they who hedge about judgment, doing righteousness at all time."*

Psalm 119:11; *"I have hid your saying in my heart, that I might not sin against you."*

Matthew 5:3; *"Blessed are the poor in spirit, because theirs is the kingdom of heaven."*

They cannot make out that Paul's doctrine is not true. For seeing that the qualities thus extolled never all so exist in man as to obtain for him the approbation of God, it follows, that man is always miserable until he is exempted from misery by the pardon of his sins.

Since, then, all the kinds of blessedness extolled in the Scripture are vain so that man derives no benefit from them until he obtains blessedness by the forgiveness of sins, a forgiveness which makes way for them, it follows that this is not only the chief and highest, but the only blessedness, unless you are prepared to maintain that it is impaired by things which owe their entire existence to it. There is much less to trouble us in the name of righteous which is usually given to believers.

However when Paul makes reference to Jews and Gentiles in common with unrighteousness, he descends to particulars and says, that "as many as have sinned without law shall also perish without law," referring to the Gentiles, and that "as many as have sinned in the law shall be judged by the law," referring to the Jews.

Moreover, as they, winking at their transgressions, boasted merely of the law, he adds most appropriately, that the law was passed with the view of justifying not those who only heard it, but those only who obeyed it; as if he had said, Do you seek righteousness in the law?

Do not bring forward the mere hearing of it, which is in itself of little weight, but bring works by which you may show that the law has not been given to you in vain.

Since in these they were all deficient, it followed that they had no ground of boasting in the law. Paul's meaning, therefore, rather leads to an opposite argument. The righteousness of the law consists in the perfection of works; but no man can boast of fulfilling the law by works, and, therefore, there is no righteousness by the law.

They now betake themselves to those passages in which believers boldly submit their righteousness to the judgment of God, and wish to be judged accordingly; as in the following passages: "Judge me, O Lord, according to my righteousness, and according to mine integrity that is in me."

Again, "Hear the right, O Lord;" "Thou hast proved mine heart; thou hast visited me in the night; thou hast tried me, and shalt find nothing."

Again "The Lord regarded me according to my righteousness; according to the cleanness of my hands has he recompensed me. For I have kept the ways of the Lord, and have not wickedly departed from my God." "I was also upright before him, and I kept myself from mine iniquity." Again, "Judge me, O Lord; for I have walked in mine integrity;" "I have not sat with vain persons; neither will I go in with dissemblers;" "Gather not my soul with sinners, nor my life with bloody men; in whose hands is mischief, and their right hand is full of bribes. But as for me, I will walk in mine integrity."

But when the saints implore the divine justice in vindication of their innocence, they do not present themselves as free from fault, and in every respect blameless but while placing their confidence of salvation in the divine goodness only, and trusting that he will vindicate his poor when they are afflicted contrary to justice and equity, they truly commit to him the cause in which the innocent are oppressed.

And when they themselves with their adversaries at the tribunal of God, they pretend not to an innocence corresponding to the divine purity were inquiry strictly made, but knowing that in comparison of the malice, dishonesty, craft, and iniquity of their enemies, their sincerity justice, simplicity, and purity, are ascertained and approved by God, they dread not to call upon him to judge between them.

Thus when David said to Saul in 1 Samuel 26:23, "*The Lord render to every man his righteousness and his faithfulness,"*, he meant not that the Lord should examine and reward every one according to his deserts, but he took the Lord to witness how great his innocence was in comparison of Saul's injustice.

Paul, too, when he indulges in the boast in 2 Corinthians 1:12, *"Our rejoicing is this, the testimony of our conscience, that in simplicity and godly sincerity, not with fleshly wisdom, but by the grace of God, we have had our conversation in the world, and more abundantly to you-ward,"*, means not to call for the scrutiny of God, but compelled by the calumnies of the wicked he appeals, in contradiction of all their slanders, to his faith and probity, which he knew that God had indulgently accepted.

For we see how he elsewhere says in 1 Corinthians 4:4, *"I know nothing by myself; yet am I not hereby justified,"*; in other words, he was aware that the divine judgment far transcended the blind estimate of man.

Therefore, however believers may, in defending their integrity against the hypocrisy of the ungodly, appeal to God as their witness and judge, still when the question is with God alone, they all with one mouth exclaim, "If thou, Lord, should mark iniquities, O Lord, who shall stand?" Again, "Enter not into judgment with thy servant; for in thy sight shall no man living be justified." Distrusting their own words, they gladly exclaim, "Thy loving-kindness is better than life,"

Yet let one of the sons of Adam come forward with such integrity. If there is none, they must perish from the presence of God, or retake themselves to the asylum of mercy. Still we deny not that the integrity of believers, though partial and imperfect, is a step to immortality. How so, but just that the works of those whom the Lord has assumed into the covenant of grace, he tries not by their merit, but embraces with paternal indulgence.

By this we understand not with the Schoolmen, that works derive their value from accepting grace. For their meaning is, that works otherwise unfit to obtain salvation in terms of law, are made fit for such a purpose by the divine acceptance. On the other hand, I maintain that these works being sullied both by other transgressions and by their own deficiencies, have no other value than this, that the Lord indulgently pardons them; in other words, that the righteousness which he bestows on man is gratuitous.

Therefore we shall never reach this goal until we have laid aside the body of sin, and been completely united to the Lord.

May he come quickly!

Conclusion

In concluding we must remember that The Law of God will never pass away, for it is written in Mat 5:17-18; *"Do not suppose that I came to loosen down the law or the prophets; I absolutely did not come to loosen down, but to fulfil. Because, Amen, I say to you, Until heaven and earth pass away, one iota or one particle will absolutely not pass away from the law until all comes to be."*

And includes every word spoken by Jesus and the Apostles to explain it,

Mat 7:12; *"Therefore all things whatever you will that men should do to you, even so you also do to them, because this is the law and the prophets."*

Its heart is love,

Mat 22:40; *"In these two commandments hang all the law and the prophets."*

It was never contradicted by Jesus or the Apostles, but they contradicted only the Pharisees' wrong understanding of the Law,

Acts 6:13; *"And they stood false witnesses, saying, This man absolutely does not stop speaking words of blasphemy against this holy place and the law,"*

Acts 18:13; *"Saying that, He incites men to worship God contrary to the law."*

The law prophesied as also the prophets prophesied,

Mat 11:13; *"Because all the prophets and the law prophesied until John."*

Devout men in the apostolic age obeyed the Law,

Acts 22:12; *"And a certain Ananias, a devout man according to the law, having a good testimony of all the Jews dwelling there,"*

Acts 24:14; *"But this I confess to you, that according to the way which they call a party, so I officially minister to the God of my fathers, believing all things according to the written law and prophets;"*

Acts 25:8; *"Defending himself, he said, Absolutely not against the law of the Jews, and absolutely not against the temple, and absolutely not against Caesar, have I sinned anything."*

The Apostles preached only out of the Law and the Prophets, because they wrote the Gospels, the Acts, the Epistles, and the Revelation; God's Law was not only given to Moses and Israel upon tablets of stone, but also written in the hearts of all men upon the face of the earth,

Rom 2:15; *"Who show the work of the law written in their hearts, their conscience witnessing with them, and their calculations between one another formally charging them or else defending them,"*

No flesh can be justified by the law, but all men come to the knowledge of sin by the Law,

Rom 3:20; *"On this very account, out of the deeds of the law there will absolutely no flesh be justified before his face, because through the law is full knowledge of sin."*

Rom 5:20; *"And law came in alongside that the transgression might abound. But where sin abounded, grace super-abounded,"*

Paul is horrified at the suggestion that he would make void the Law,

Rom 3:31, *"Therefore do we render the law inoperative through faith? We do not! On the contrary, we cause the law to stand."*

So he establishes it; we are not free from the Law, but free from sin and guilt of violating the Law,

Rom 6:18, *"And being made free from sin, you were made servants of righteousness."*

Rom 6: 22; *"And now being set free from sin and made servants to God, you have your fruit into holiness, and the end everlasting life,"*

Rom 7:3-4; *"So therefore if, the husband living, she is to another man, according to divine oracle she is an adulteress, and if the husband dies she is free from that law, so that, being to another man, she is not an adulteress.*
Therefore, my brothers, you also were made dead to the law through the body of Christ, into becoming married to another, to the one raised out of the dead, that we may bear fruit to God,"

Rom 8:2; *"Because the law of the Spirit of life in Christ Jesus has set me free from the law of sin and death,"*

The fleshly mind is not subject to the Law,

Rom 8:7, *"On this very account the fleshly mind is hostile against God, because it absolutely will not arrange itself under the law of God, because it absolutely does not have the power."*

But the mind renewed by the Holy Spirit fulfils the Law,

Rom 8:4; *"That the righteous deeds of the law might be fulfilled in us, who walk not according to the flesh, but according to the Spirit,"*

Rom13:8, *"Do not owe anyone anything, except to love one another, because the one loving another has fulfilled the law,"*

Rom 13:10; *"Love absolutely does not work any evil to his neighbour; love therefore is the fulfilment of the law."*

No man can be saved by our works of the Law,

Gal 2:16, *"Having seen that a man is absolutely not justified out of law works, but through Jesus Christ's faith, we also have believed into Jesus Christ, so that we may be justified out of Christ's faith, and absolutely not out of law works, because out of law works absolutely no flesh will be justified."*

Gal 2:21; *"I absolutely do not set aside the grace of God, because if righteousness is through the law, then Christ is dead for nothing."*

Gal 3:10-12, *"Because as many as are out of law works are under a curse, because it has been*

written, Cursed is everyone who absolutely does not continue in all things which are written in the scroll of the law to do them.
11 And that absolutely no one is justified in the law alongside of God, it is clear, because, The righteous will live out of faith.
12 And the law is absolutely not out of faith, but, The man doing them shall live in them."

And Christ has redeemed us from the curse of the Law,

Gal 3:14-15; *"That the blessing of Abraham might be to the races in Christ Jesus, that we might take the promise of the Spirit through faith. Brothers, I speak according to man, Even a man's covenant made authoritative, absolutely no one sets aside, or adds to it."*

The Law is not against the promises of God,

Gal 3:21; *"Is the law therefore against the promises of God? It shall not be, because if there had been a law given which had power to make alive, truly righteousness would have been out of the law."*

The Law is the servant bringing us to Christ,

Gal 3:24; *"Thus the law was our guardian into Christ, that we might be justified out of faith."*

Anyone trying to save himself by the Law falls short of reaching grace,

Gal 5:14; *"Because all the law is fulfilled in the one word: You shall love your neighbor as yourself."*

The Law is beautifully good, if we use it lawfully,

1 Tim 1:8; *"And we see that the law is beautifully good, if anyone uses it lawfully."*

What Saint Paul was fighting against was a wrong use of the Law by people in their attempt to save themselves by good works rather than trusting Jesus the fulfilment of the Law.

The only parts of the Law not completely stated again in the New Covenant as binding upon all believers are the dietary laws and the Sabbath laws.

These are left to the individual judgment of the believer as to whether or not he will keep those.

Col 2:16; *"Therefore do not let anyone judge you in food, or in drink, or in sharing of a festival, or a new moon festival, or of the Sabbaths,"*

Amen

Bibliography and References

1. http://www.frame-poythress.org/frame_articles/2002Law.htm

2. http://www.girs.com/library/theology/syllabus/nom1.html

3. Westminster Confession of Faith XIX

4. http://thedevilsplan.blogspot.com

5 http://www.ccel.org/ccel/anonymous/westminster3.pdf

6. http://www.ceremoniallaw.com/

7. http://www.founders.org/FJ28/article1.html

8. Charles Bridges, The Christian Ministry, London: Banner of Truth Trust, 1967

9. http://en.wikipedia.org/wiki/Antinomian

10. http://homepage.mac.com/shanerosenthal/reformationink/relawgospel.htm

11. http://www.spurgeon.org/sermons/0037.htm

12. John Bunyan, The Pilgrims Progress Cathedral University Press

13. Watchman Nee, The Law of This Spirit of Life Wikipedia online encyclopaedia

14. http://www.ccel.org/ccel/calvin/institutes.iv.x.html

15. http://www.ccel.org/ccel/calvin/institutes.v.xviii.html

16. The Heritage Bible

17. King James Version Bible

18. The New International Version Bible

www.ingramcontent.com/pod-product-compliance
Ingram Content Group UK Ltd.
Pitfield, Milton Keynes, MK11 3LW, UK
UKHW041941190726
13854UKWH00004B/1729